ENCYCLOPEDIA OF MAMMALS

VOLUME 13
Rat–Sea

MARSHALL CAVENDISH

NEW YORK • LONDON • TORONTO • SYDNEY

RAT KANGAROOS

Dave Watts/ANT/NHPA

HOPPERS AND BOUNDERS

DIMINUTIVE COUSINS OF THE LARGER KANGAROOS, TODAY'S RAT KANGAROOS REPRESENT THE EARLY STAGES IN THE EVOLUTION OF AUSTRALIA'S FAMOUS BIG-FOOTED MARSUPIALS

In a land full of wildlife curiosities, Australia is renowned perhaps above all for its marsupials adapted for moving around on two legs. Kangaroos and wallabies are the most famous, but less well known are the miniatures of the type, the mammals known as rat kangaroos. Although much smaller and more compact in form, they share that most kangaroo-like of kangaroo features: enlargement of the hind legs into limbs built for hopping.

Among the first animal species recorded when Europeans began to explore Australia—the long-nosed potoroo was described in 1789—rat kangaroos have suffered terribly over the last two centuries. Nearly all species have declined into rarity, and two, the broad-faced potoroo and the desert rat kangaroo, are now pronounced extinct. But scarce though most may be, their biology and behavior still give us a key insight into the origins and evolution of Australia's most distinctive marsupial lineage.

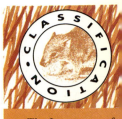

The kangaroos and rat kangaroos of today share an ancestry of great age. For tens of millions of years their ancestors gradually evolved alongside the distantly related possums, and then about thirty million years ago species started to diversify rapidly. The fossil record of the time shows the development of various forms of primitive animals, most of them clearly forerunners of present-day rat kangaroos. The development of animals similar to today's larger kangaroos took place much later.

THE MUSK RAT KANGAROO

First to flourish were a group of marsupials represented today by the smallest and least kangaroo-like of species, the musk rat kangaroo. It may be that a creature similar to the musk rat kangaroo evolved from rain-forest possums that became adapted for living on the forest floor. Certain features of both the ancestors and the modern-day animal are similar to those in possums, including the presence of a mobile first toe on the hind feet and the complex brain. Although the musk rat kangaroo has longer hind limbs than forelimbs, the difference between them is not much greater than in ringtail possums. On the ground the animal moves on all fours.

In many other ways, too, the musk rat kangaroo differs from the rest of its family. It still inhabits dense rain-forest habitats where it is an adept

Dave Watts/ANT/NHPA

A bettong shepherds her youngster through the leaf litter of Tasmania's forests (above).

Babs & Bert Wells/Oxford Scientific Films

*in*SIGHT

THE HONEY POSSUM

Despite its name, the honey possum is only distantly related to the true possums. With a head-and-body length of less than 4 in (10 cm) but a thin, strongly prehensile tail of at least the same length, it has a pointed snout and a long, brush-tipped tongue. Using its gripping feet and tail, it climbs easily among the foliage of the heaths and shrubs in southwestern Australia.

Though there are other marsupials that feed on nectar and pollen, none seems to rely so completely on these sources of food as the honey possum. This diet suggests that the honey possum lineage flourished about twenty million years ago when the rich Australian heathlands were in their heyday. Since then the heaths have contracted, and we are left with a sole descendant in a corner of the continent. Interestingly, the sperm produced by the male are the largest known in any mammal.

climber; it possesses a simple stomach and has a more easily digestible diet; and it is the only species that gives birth to two young.

TAKING TO THE GROUND

By the mid-Miocene epoch (fifteen million years ago), new forms had become more prevalent in Australia—groups of animals represented today by the other members of the rat kangaroo family, such as the potoroos, bettongs, rufous rat kangaroo, and desert rat kangaroo. In these animals the typical kangaroo body plan was clearly taking shape. The climbing ability provided by similar-sized limbs and flexible, grasping hind feet was sacrificed. The hind legs were now much longer and more powerful than the forelegs, and the lengthened hind feet, along with the thicker tail, were becoming the animal's props, leaving the forefeet for digging and grasping food.

The modern descendants of these animals all move on two feet with slow hops or fast bounds. Some, like the long-nosed potoroo, place their forelimbs on the ground when foraging or to help change direction when fleeing, but propulsion for the movements comes from the hind limbs.

The early rat kangaroos developed their distinctive gait in more open habitats, where they ate different foods from rain-forest animals. Since the

The honey possum feeds on pollen and nectar, which it licks up with its long, bristly tongue.

continent was becoming drier, wooded or grassy habitats were on the increase at the expense of forests, providing ample but coarser vegetable food. To cope better with the digestive demands of such foodstuffs, rat kangaroos developed more complex, multichambered stomachs where the breakdown of tough food could be prolonged.

By the start of the Pliocene epoch (five million years ago) these ancestral rat kangaroos were finally being eclipsed by the next group in line. With the climate still drying out and the land becoming more open, the stage was set for larger, swifter grazers and browsers. The wallabies and kangaroos emerged on the evolutionary scene and rapidly became the dominant terrestrial plant-eaters.

Though rat kangaroos and "proper" kangaroos share many key features, the differences between the two families are also quite distinct. Rat kangaroos are not only smaller, being roughly rabbit-sized, but are also more compact in shape. Key differences are also present in the bones of the skull and in the shapes and arrangement of the teeth. ∎

THE RAT KANGAROO'S FAMILY TREE

It seems that the ancestors of the primitive honey possum branched away from other diprotodonts at a very early stage. Successive branchings led to the wombats and koala, then to the possum families, and finally to a split between the ancestors of today's rat kangaroos and their larger, more familiar cousins, the wallabies and kangaroos.

HONEY POSSUM

Tarsipedidae
(tar-see-PED-ee-die)

This small, shrewlike marsupial is the only member of its family. With its very long, sparsely haired and prehensile tail, it is adapted for climbing into vegetation and feeding from blossoms using the narrow, tubular snout and long, extendable tongue. The honey possum inhabits heaths and shrub country in southwest Australia, where it is active mainly at night.

B/W Illustrations Ruth Grewcock

BILBIES

MARSUPIAL CARNIVORES

AMERICAN OPOSSUMS

POLYPROTODONTS

MARSUPIAL MOLES

BANDICOOTS

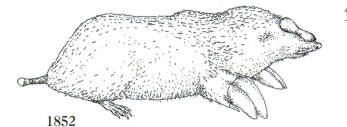

RAT KANGAROOS

Potoroidae
(*pot-o-RO-id-ie*)

There are ten species of rat kangaroos found in a wide range of habitats. They are generally larger than most possums but smaller and more crouching than the wallabies. All but the musk rat kangaroo have long hind limbs and move quickly with a hopping gait. Most species have a long tail, which is thickened at the base but less well furred than the body. They feed mainly on vegetable matter, although some species also eat invertebrates. They are mainly nocturnal and seldom social.

Color illustrations Dan Wright

CUSCUSES AND
BRUSHTAILS

GLIDERS

KANGAROOS AND
WALLABIES

DIPROTODONTS

WOMBATS

KOALA

PYGMY POSSUMS

ALL MARSUPIALS

ANATOMY:
THE RAT KANGAROO

The largest rat kangaroo is the burrowing bettong (above right), with an average head-and-body length of 15.5 in (394 mm) and a tail length of about 12 in (305 mm). The honey possum (above left) measures only 2.5–3.3 in (64–84 mm) from head to rump and has a tail length of 2.7–4 in (69–102 mm).

THE FORELIMBS

are short but powerful. They may provide some support when the animal is moving slowly but are not really used for locomotion. Instead they are free for grasping food and for digging roots from the ground.

THE FOREFEET

have five digits, each equipped with a long, curved claw. The hind feet are long and rigid, the first hind toe is missing, and the second and third are fused to form a sharp-clawed digit that is used for grooming. The long fourth and fifth toes play a key part in locomotion.

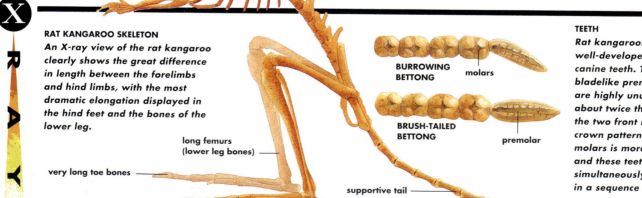

X

X-RAY

RAT KANGAROO SKELETON

An X-ray view of the rat kangaroo clearly shows the great difference in length between the forelimbs and hind limbs, with the most dramatic elongation displayed in the hind feet and the bones of the lower leg.

long femurs (lower leg bones)

very long toe bones

BURROWING BETTONG — molars

BRUSH-TAILED BETTONG

premolar

supportive tail

TEETH

Rat kangaroos possess well-developed upper canine teeth. Their bladelike premolars (left) are highly unusual, being about twice the length of the two front molars. The crown pattern of the molars is more uneven, and these teeth emerge simultaneously rather than in a sequence over time.

X-ray illustrations Elisabeth Smith

BURROWING BETTONG FEET

The burrowing bettong is the only "big-footed" member of the family known to live in burrows on a regular basis. The long-clawed forefeet are used for burrowing and digging up foodstuffs, while the long hind feet propel it along. The tail is used in support only when the animal is stationary.

FOREFOOT

HIND FOOT

CLASSIFICATION

GENUS: *AEPYPRYMNUS*
SPECIES: *RUFESCENS*

SIZE

HEAD–BODY LENGTH: 15–15.5 IN (38–39 CM)
TAIL LENGTH: 13.5–15.5 IN (34–39 CM)
WEIGHT: 6.5–7.5 LB (3–3.4 KG)

COLORATION

REDDISH BROWN TO GRAY-BROWN; WHITISH UNDERPARTS

FEATURES

HIND LIMBS LONGER THAN FORELIMBS
GRIZZLED FUR
HAIRY SNOUT (UNLIKE OTHER SPECIES)
POINTED EARS
THICK, LONG, AND PREHENSILE TAIL
LARGEST OF THE RAT KANGAROOS

THE COAT
of the rufous rat kangaroo is coarse and the reddish color is often flecked with gray; this gives the animal a grizzled appearance.

THE TAIL
is long and thick. It acts both as a prop when the animal is resting or moving slowly and as a counterbalance when it is hopping fast. Because it is prehensile, the rat kangaroo can use it to carry fresh grass for its nest.

RAT KANGAROO SKULL *(LEFT)*
The skull of the rufous rat kangaroo is quite broad but tapers forward to the narrow snout. Prominent eye sockets house the fairly large eyes, adapted for nighttime vision.

HONEY POSSUM SKULL (RIGHT)

finely tapering snout

HONEY POSSUM SKELETON
The honey possum's bones are lightweight, enabling it to clamber upon flower heads. The long, muscular tail is able to grip supports. The skull (left) has a very long, tapering snout; the teeth are small and curved and the palate is equipped with hard ridges. This dentition enables the possum to scrape nectar off its long tongue.

lightweight, agile frame

prehensile tail

Main illustration Steve Kingston

TIMID FORAGERS

SMALL, SHY, FOND OF DENSE COVER, AND ACTIVE UNDER THE CANOPY OF DARKNESS, THE RAT KANGAROOS ARE FAR LESS LIKELY TO BE SPOTTED IN THE WILD THAN SOME OF THEIR MORE BULKY RELATIVES

I f it were not for their style of movement, it might be difficult to accept that rat kangaroos are related to the larger kangaroos of Australia. The conspicuous and sociable tendencies of the latter contrast sharply with the skulking, largely solitary nature of their diminutive cousins.

One of the many differences in the behavior routine of the rat kangaroos is their daily retreat into shelter. Except for the musk rat kangaroo, which is active in the hours of early morning and late afternoon and rests at night, all the rat kangaroos are busy at night and lie up in shelter throughout the day. The long-nosed potoroo may start feeding just before dark and is occasionally at large in full daylight, but all others are strictly nocturnal and can only be spotted by day when they are flushed from cover. The honey possum, likewise, is fully nocturnal—one side-effect of this can be seen in its limited range of vocal and visual communication signals.

DAY NESTS

The lengths to which they go to secure adequate shelter are remarkable. Bettongs and the rufous rat kangaroo construct their own nests of grass, sticks, and bark, the nesting material carried to the base of a bush or tall tussock in the animal's prehensile tail. The dome- or cone-shaped nest has an entrance and is often built over a shallow excavation.

The burrowing bettong takes over an old rabbit warren or actually digs out a burrow in the earth. Using its clawed forelimbs, it excavates a simple tunnel for itself with one or two entrances, or combines with others of its kind to make a complex, interconnecting warren with many entrances, deep tunnels, and nesting chambers. Potoroos, by contrast, sleep among simple piles of grass placed over scrapes, while the musk rat kangaroo takes nighttime shelter in clumps of vines or between tree buttresses.

When the hour is right, rat kangaroos emerge from their shelter to begin bouts of foraging. The musk rat kangaroo makes its way nervously over the forest floor on all fours, making small "bunny hops," with the forefeet placed down and the hind feet moved forward together under its body. It also climbs up onto fallen trunks and branches. Potoroos and the rufous rat kangaroo may also forage with the forefeet in contact with the ground, although their function is merely to take the animal's weight while it pushes its hind legs forward. The burrowing bettong, on the other hand, never uses its forefeet in locomotion, even when ambling.

Rates of activity among rat kangaroos vary. While some, such as the brush-tailed bettong, forage quite slowly, others, such as the long-nosed potoroo,

A Tasmanian bettong in full flight (above) *hunches down and tucks in its forepaws.*

TAIL TRAVEL

Rat kangaroos still have a flexible, prehensile-tipped tail like their distant tree-climbing ancestors. Though the animals no longer need it for climbing, they put the gripping ability to excellent use when building their nests. After gathering and shredding material such as grass in its mouth, the bettong places the pile on the ground and curls it up in its tail. Gripped into a compact bundle, the grass is then carried either to a new nest site or to refurbish an old one. A bettong may use the same nest for a month or so, keeping it in good condition by lifting up old material with its long snout and transferring new grass underneath.

are very active. Given its long fur, this potoroo needs an outlet for excess body heat when exercising, and it is unusual in being able to sweat profusely from its naked tail. Indeed, it is the smallest of all mammals known to sweat.

SWIFT IN DEFENSE

Rat kangaroos have good senses of sight and hearing and remain ever alert when they are out foraging, ready to rush for cover when danger threatens. Typical enemies include foxes, dingoes, cats, marsupial carnivores like the quoll or native cat, as well as pythons and large hawks. Though they do not all move very fast, rat kangaroos can make agile twists and turns, and sometimes execute darting double-backs to throw pursuers off their trail. The musk rat kangaroo flees with a four-legged galloping motion, but all other species hop and bound on their powerful hind legs, usually with the tail held out, body angled forward, head held low, and forefeet withdrawn. Potoroos make use of their forefeet when moving fast, but only to assist them in changing direction.

Some rat kangaroos have surprisingly high stamina. A fleeing desert rat kangaroo was reported to have exhausted two galloping horses in a long chase across the scrub. Rat kangaroos also have the power to react to sudden danger with a prodigious leap. Propelled by the hind legs, potoroos can make an initial bound 8.5 ft (2.6 m) long and 5 ft (1.5 m) high, enough to spring out of immediate danger when they are disturbed in the nest. ■

The tiny honey possum is so light that it can perch on flower heads to feed, aided by its gripping tail.

HABITATS

The range of habitats occupied by rat kangaroos, at least until recent times, encompassed almost the full variety of habitats in the Australian continent, from lush rain forest to the arid interior. The dramatic decline in distribution of several species means that some former habitats are no longer in use, yet still the range for the family remains great.

Just as it differs in so many anatomical respects, so the musk rat kangaroo stands apart from its relatives in its choice of habitat. It is the only species to be found in the tropical rain forests of northern Queensland, occupying pockets of dense forest on the coastal lowland and in the uplands to altitudes of 5,000 ft (1,500 m). It seems to prefer the dampest

---

EUCALYPTUS TREES PROBABLY ORIGINATED IN AUSTRALIA'S PRIMEVAL TROPICAL RAIN FORESTS

---

sites within its luxuriant haunt and often lives close to creeks and rivers. The rain forests are believed to have existed in northeastern Australia for tens of millions of years. Today's relics of once much more extensive forests have therefore acted as a refuge for some equally ancient lineages. Insulated from the pressures of a changing environment, some of the species in them retain highly primitive characteristics. Not only the home of the ratlike musk rat

DISTRIBUTION

The region of greatest species diversity is the humid strip in the east and southeast; parts of this area are home to the rufous and musk rat kangaroos, the northern bettong, and the long-nosed and long-footed potoroos. The Tasmanian bettong now occurs only on Tasmania. Elsewhere, the burrowing bettong is found today on a few islands off the western coast, and the brush-tailed bettong survives in pockets in the southwest corner. The southwest was also the home of the now extinct broad-faced potoroo, while the desert rat kangaroo once occupied a limited region of central Australia.

KEY

- MUSK RAT KANGAROO
- DESERT RAT KANGAROO
- POTOROOS
- BETTONGS
- HONEY POSSUM
- RUFOUS RAT KANGAROO

Rudie H. Kuiter/Oxford Scientific Films

inSIGHT

OUT OF THE FLAMES

Natural fires, though at times terrifying in their seemingly destructive power, play a key part in the natural history of Australia. Studies have shown that the brush-tailed bettong in particular benefits from the effect of fire on its habitat. For those living in the dry woodlands of the southwest, wildfires every several years or so maintain the ground layer of heartleaf thickets. Fire stimulates the plants' seeds to germinate, providing fresh growth and shelter, but at the same time thins the cover enough to make it easy to traverse. Fire also triggers the growth of the bettong's favorite food—underground fungi that develop in the soil around the thickets.

kangaroo, the rain forests are also host to the most ancestral looking of possums, the green ringtail, and what may be the most primitive form of flowering plant today: a magnolia whose pollen is nearly identical to fossil pollen 120 million years old.

POTOROOS

The two living species of potoroos occur farther south, well outside the tropical zone, but they too tend to occur in densely wooded terrain, including temperate rain forest, eucalyptus woodlands, and coastal heathlands. Though their preferred habitats are not nearly as humid or as closed canopy as those of the musk rat kangaroo, they seldom occur outside areas that experience at least 30 in (760 mm) average rainfall—places damp enough to support extensive woody cover. In addition, potoroos seem highly reliant on dense ground cover, such as shrubs, grasses, sedges, or ferns. They are also most concentrated in areas where the soil is light and crumbly, enabling them to dig easily for food.

The now-extinct broad-faced potoroo had a very different home. It lived mainly in open, grassy habitats farther inland from the wooded zones of the southwest. In this respect it had more in common with the other members of the family—animals that tend to live in drier, more open habitats. The rufous rat kangaroo, for example, lives in open woodlands

with plenty of tall grass growing in the abundant sunlight that reaches the floor. The Tasmanian bettong occupies a similar type of habitat, although its former distribution on the mainland was largely open plains country, and the brush-tailed bettong prefers open woodland with clumped ground vegetation of scrub or grass tussocks.

DRYLAND DIGGER

While the last two species avoid areas of truly dense vegetation, they both require a reasonable amount of ground cover. This is not the case for the burrowing bettong, whose ability to survive in sparsely vegetated terrain allowed it to occupy open habitats across the dry interior of the continent. One of its principal requirements was soil deep enough and firm enough for burrowing, and it often chose sites around rocky outcrops or under boulders. The burrowing bettong still survives on rocky islands, but the final member of the family, the desert rat kangaroo, had no such refuges. It was perhaps the most hardy of the family, living in one of the hottest, driest parts of the interior—a stony terrain of plains, sand ridges, and claypans scantily clad with scattered shrubs such as saltbush and emu bush.

The need for shelter both from the elements and from predators becomes more intense the more open the habitat. The burrowing bettong has

The brush-tailed bettong inhabits open-forest regions where the ground cover features tussock grasses or low shrubs. It spends its nights hopping in typical hunched fashion (right) *in search of fungi and plant parts on the woodland floor.*

Babs & Bert Wells/Oxford Scientific Films

evolved a neat solution to both. Safe inside its burrow when resting, it finds shade and cooler air temperatures underground away from the searing daytime temperatures on the surface. The desert rat kangaroo was not a burrower, but it braved the daytime elements as best as it could by building a complex nest on the surface, complete with a side entrance and a peephole in the roof for surveying the surroundings for approaching danger.

The complexity of nest-building lessens as species' habitats become less dry and offer more standing vegetation cover. The potoroos need create only simple refuges because the density of ground foliage allows them concealment from enemies, and the sunshine reaching the ground in their more humid haunts is less intense. Indeed, the long-nosed potoroo has to cope instead with regularly cool conditions in parts of its range, and its fairly long fur may be there to provide insulation.

One further environmental hazard common for many Australian animals is the threat of being caught in bushfires. Wildfires sweep from time to time even through humid woodland, and small, ground-dwelling animals can easily become caught in the flames. The long-nosed potoroo is sometimes forced to take shelter in the burrows of other animals. Eucalyptus fires in particular are devastating

M. Harvey/Natural Science Photos. Inset ANT/NHPA

FOCUS ON

NORTHERN QUEENSLAND RAIN FORESTS

In terms of the luxuriance of their vegetation and animal life, the tropical rain forests along the coast of northern Queensland are the richest habitats in all Australia. Though they occupy only a tiny part of the continent's land area—a fraction of one percent—they are home to nearly a fifth of Australian bird species, 30 percent of its marsupials, and some 60 percent of its butterflies. Hundreds of tree species intermingle to form the forest's canopy, among them ebony, paperbark, laurels, and a range of eucalypts. Fan palms, figs, vines, and ferns are abundant, and the forests harbor some one hundred orchids, many of them anchored to tree trunks and branches.

Some of the plants and animals of the rain forests have spread across from the forests of Southeast Asia ever since Australia's northerly tectonic drift brought it into close enough proximity. They include rodents and bats and colorful forest birds such as paradise kingfishers and pittas. New Guinea meanwhile has provided its neighbor with a few species of cuscuses, tree kangaroos, bowerbirds, and birds of paradise.

TEMPERATURE AND RAINFALL

■ TEMPERATURE

■ RAINFALL

Tropical rain forests flourish where there is stable warmth and high rainfall throughout the year. Mean annual temperature in the Australian forests is about 73°F (23°C), and average annual rainfall is about 156 in (4,000 mm).

in their ferocity and in the rapidity with which they spread; this is due to the highly combustible oil in the leaves, which virtually explodes when ignited.

But fire has its positive impacts on the ecosystem, too (see Out of the Flames, page 1858). Along with unevenness of terrain and variations in soil type and moisture, it helps to create vegetation variety and patchiness in the environment. Many rat kangaroos thrive best where there is a mosaic of vegetation, providing more open places for foraging and denser patches for shelter. ■

NEIGHBORS

The leafy, moist Queensland forests are refuges for both Australian and New Guinean mammals, and the sun-dappled canopy flashes with the lustrous plumage of tropical birds.

ECLECTUS PARROT

The green plumage of the male eclectus gives good camouflage; the female is a vivid crimson.

TREE KANGAROO

Bennet's tree kangaroo is arboreal; it has strong forelimbs and sharp claws to help it climb.

Neighbor illustrations Robin Carter/Wildlife Art Agency

NORTHERN QUEENSLAND

The tropical rain forests of coastal northern Queensland are home to the musk rat kangaroo. This species prefers the moist regions close to creeks and rivers, where it forages among the leaf litter for fruits and insects.

MUSK RAT KANGAROO

Great Barrier Reef

QUEENSLAND

FRILLED LIZARD

The colorful neck ruffle of the Australian frilled lizard is erected to intimidate would-be predators.

FERAL PIG

Feral pigs, descendants of livestock that escaped long ago, roam the forests in groups of up to twenty.

RAINBOW BEE-EATER

This delightful bird is a deft catcher of flying insects. It gathers in large flocks throughout the year.

BENT-WING BAT

Common bent-wing bats roost in the thousands in caverns, emerging after sundown to hunt for insects.

RUFOUS OWL

The rufous owl hunts small mammals, including rat kangaroos, in rain forest and dense woodland.

TERRITORY

Where rat kangaroos still occur, suitable habitats can support fairly high populations of the animals. Average densities of over one individual per acre (2.5 per hectare) have been recorded for the long-nosed potoroo, and in many species figures of one animal for every five to ten acres (one for every two to four hectares) are normal across areas of suitable habitat. Even in such places, however, rat kangaroos—with one exception—are markedly unsocial in their habits. Rat kangaroos are basically solitary animals, unlike many of their larger cousins. Adults tend to nest and forage alone, and two animals seen in close company for any length of time are likely to be a female and her dependent young.

LIVING ALONE

A single musk rat kangaroo keeps to a small patch of forest and seldom interacts with its neighbors except when seeking to mate. Occasionally two or three of the animals may be seen feeding at the same site, perhaps where there is a lot of fallen fruit, but the meeting seems only coincidental.

In prime habitat, long-nosed potoroos occupy small home ranges, but in less favorable sites the size is likely to be closer 50 acres (20 hectares) for males and 12.5 acres (5 hectares) for females. These ranges are not exclusive and at times small groups of animals feed together, but nesting is always alone.

Brush-tailed bettongs can be ferocious in defense of their home range; these two (right) *are fighting over territory.*

COLONIES

of burrowing bettongs (below) *dig complex warrens into dryland soil, often siting them around boulders. Some burrows are also made in the floors of caves.*

DIGGING DEEP

Armed with its sharp foreclaws, the burrowing bettong is a proficient digger (right). *It prefers light, crumbly soil but can make do in firmly packed terrain in arid regions.*

The ranges of male long-nosed potoroos often overlap with those of several females, reflecting the species' tendency to breed promiscuously. But although females seem to tolerate sharing ranges with one another, males do so less frequently. In the long-footed potoroo, a seemingly monogamous species, overlaps in home ranges are allowed only between established partners.

Most other species of rat kangaroos have a social structure similar to that of the long-nosed potoroo. Rufous rat kangaroos occupy extensively overlapping home ranges of about 50 acres (20 hectares), with a cluster of day nests used on an alternating basis by a single animal in the middle of each range. Loose gatherings of rufous rat kangaroos often feed in company at prime food sources, communicating with growls and grunts.

BRUSH-TAILED DEFENDER

The brush-tailed bettong, like the rufous rat kangaroo, has a large home range in keeping with its less resource-rich habitat, but within this lies a core feeding territory of 10–22.5 acres (4–9 hectares). The core area not only contains the individual's principal food resources, but also three or four current nests—the sites of which are actively defended against intruders, especially by males against other males.

A brush-tailed bettong's attachment to its core territory is so strong that it may refuse to abandon it even during bushfires. Instead of fleeing, the animal has been seen to move calmly ahead of the advancing line of flames. If, by the time the bettong has been pushed to the edge of its territory, it has not found refuge, such as an old burrow, the animal simply bounds back through the flames and smoke to the charred terrain behind.

The Tasmanian bettong has the largest living space of all rat kangaroos. In some cases individuals have occupied home ranges up to 340 acres (138 hectares) in size, and they are quite ready to travel 1 mile (1.6 km) between the nest and their nightly feeding sites. Yet the core area is still well defended. Nest sites are marked with scent from anal glands, and if necessary both sexes are prepared to fight for their home areas by biting and kicking opponents.

UNDERGROUND COMMUNITIES

The odd species out when it comes to sociability is the burrowing bettong. Though the burrowing bettong sometimes digs simple individual underground homes, it is better known for its complex communal burrows. The only rat kangaroo species that can be

---

THE TUNNELS OF BURROWING BETTONGS MAY HAVE ANY NUMBER OF ENTRANCES FROM TWO TO OVER A HUNDRED

---

described as social, this animal often lives in large groups that share the interconnected tunnel system in which they nest and take shelter. Warrens containing forty or fifty individuals are known, and on Barrow Island one commune has been found with more than 120 entrances. The burrows are dug predominantly in deep, loamy soil, but their location varies with the type of habitat. In salt lake areas, for example, bettongs burrow in rises or "islands" within the broad, flat lake pans. In sandy, undulating desert areas, however, the lower, damper areas are favored for burrowing. When above ground, the animals forage far and wide, in some cases up to three miles (4.8 km) from the burrow.

Usually the burrows are smaller, and are typically home to one adult male and several females. Groups such as this appear to be the basic social unit for this species, with males attempting to maintain relations with a set of females rather than lay strict claim to a territory above ground. Nevertheless, each male acts aggressively toward other males in defense of his "harem," whereas females are relatively peaceable. Not suprisingly, given its sociability, the burrowing bettong is the most vocal of the rat kangaroos, communicating with its associates and rivals with a range of hisses, squeals and grunts. ■

Tom McHugh/Photo Researchers/Oxford Scientific Films

Illustration Steve Roberts/Wildlife Art Agency

FOOD AND FEEDING

The honey possum leads a life of specialization. This unique little animal feeds solely on nectar and pollen, and the availability of abundant, year-round supplies strictly limits where it can live. The sandy heaths and shrublands of the Australian southwest are rich in flowering plants, with some 3,600 species. They host a high density and variety of the flower-cone–bearing shrubs that are crucial to the honey possum—both because of their abundant blooms and because of the staggered flowering seasons of different species. In this suitable habitat, the honey possum remains relatively common.

POSSUM BLOSSOMS

When out and about foraging, honey possums sometimes climb into tree branches to reach prime blossoms, but most of their activity takes place low down in the shrub layer. Agile and brisk, they dart from flower to flower with four-legged runs along branches and with tail held straight behind. They can climb vertical stems with ease and even walk upside down below branches, aided by grasping feet, spreading digits, and roughened pads on the digit tips. The prehensile tail provides further support, and by using it as a fifth limb the honey possum leaves its forefeet free for handling stems and petals. Given its tiny size and its agility, this marsupial can reach blossoms at the ends of slender twigs.

in SIGHT

FLOWER-PROBING

The honey possum not only has a long, slender snout with which to probe into flower heads, it also has an elongated tongue that is bristly at the end. Like the brush-tipped tongue of a lory—an Australian parrot that similarly feeds on nectar—this organ is an excellent aid for lapping up droplets of nectar and for licking pollen grains from the heavily laden anthers at the tips of the stamens (the male parts of the flower). With rapid movements, the honey possum collects the food on the tip of the tongue and then retracts it into the mouth, where nectar and pollen is scraped off onto the canine teeth and onto a set of hard ridges on the palate.

THE HONEY POSSUM

finds all the food it needs inside the tightly packed banksia flowers that decorate its heathland home. Climbing among the shrubs, helped by its light weight, grasping feet, and gripping tail, this tiny marsupial probes each flower for its sweet nectar and grains of pollen (right).

Illustration W. Bramall/Wildlife Art Agency

Though captive animals will accept invertebrate food, there is no evidence that wild honey possums include them on their menu. Nectar procured from flowers using the long snout and tongue provides the bulk of their diet. But nectar, though rich in sugar and easily digestible, is not enough to maintain an animal. Instead, the animal derives the proteins, amino acids, and vitamins it needs from another flower product—pollen. Pollen grains, with their tough coats, are harder to digest, but up to three days spent passing through the two stomach chambers of the honey possum are enough to ensure that most pollen grains excreted by the animal have been emptied of their nutrients.

CROSS-POLLINATION

If a honey possum ate all the pollen from a bloom, attracting the animal with nectar would be counterproductive for the plant; but this is not what happens. Enough pollen attaches to the animal's snout to make it an effective cross-pollinator on its foraging travels. This role seems sufficiently important that banksias, the plants most important to the honey possum, have evolved remarkably alluring blossoms. Their flowers are highly fragrant, produce abundant nectar and pollen, and are packed in tight clusters with stems strong enough that they can be clambered over by a small mammal.

Though there is always at least one species of banksia in bloom on the heaths at any time of the year, food shortages do develop in summer. At this time numbers of honey possums tend to fall, and dietary crises force some individuals into a short period of torpor. But when flowers are plentiful in spring, honey possums can get by with relative ease. A female constrained by nursing young can obtain all her foraging needs from an area just 33 ft (10 m) across, perhaps even centered on a single banksia shrub.

The honey possum is guided to its food source largely by the fragrance of the blooms (above).

1865

Rat kangaroos have their favorite foods, but none are dietary specialists. Depending on what is locally available, they feed on fruit, seeds, flowers, leaves, stems, bulbs, and roots. Fungi are a consistently important part of their diet, and most species consume at least a little invertebrate food.

The musk rat kangaroo forages over the forest floor and along low, sloping branches, and often eats insects. Using its forepaws to rifle through leaf litter and turn over soil, this species also uses its teeth to tear open decaying wood to find prey. It first seizes an insect, such as a grasshopper, in its teeth and then holds the prey in its forepaws to eat while

> THE BURROWING BETTONG HAS BEEN KNOWN TO FEED ON CARRION WASHED UP ON THE COASTS OF ITS ISLAND REFUGES

resting on its haunches. Most other rat kangaroos eat a few insects and other invertebrates, either deliberately or with their plant food.

Even for the musk rat kangaroo, animal food is a minor part of the diet; fallen fruit provides most of its food. Other rat kangaroos forage to varying extents for edible plant items at ground level, but, despite their more complex stomachs, few rely heavily on green growth. The rufous rat kangaroo regularly crops grasses and herbs; but for most potoroos and bettongs, stems and leaves are no more important in the diet than seeds and fruit.

BURIED TREASURE

The plant material that does play a major role lies underground. Plant roots and storage organs such as tubers are eaten regularly by most species and are probably the most important food sources for the rufous rat kangaroo and the burrowing bettong. With the exception of the musk rat kangaroo, all rat kangaroos are equipped to dig into the ground with their forefeet to extract a ready meal. The rufous rat kangaroo commonly digs beneath pasture herbs that have long taproots, while the tastes and digging ability of the burrowing bettong made it

BETTONGS

eat roots and tubers; they also nibble foliage from low grasses and herbs (right).

MUSHROOMS

attract potoroos to likely sites where they can expose fruiting fungi in the topsoil (above). *These species also dig up roots, tubers, and insects.*

Tasmanian bettongs, like all rat kangaroos, hold food in their forepaws while nibbling (left).

a serious pest on agricultural crops in the past. A burrowing bettong, probably like other species, appears to locate its food by smell, sniffing close to the ground as it forages over the surface.

FUNGUS-FEEDERS

Roots and tubers are by no means all that rat kangaroos find underground. The pits dug by potoroos, for example, often yield insect larvae and worms— but the real subterranean prize for these animals is fungi. As well as being an unusual source of food, fungus is now known to be the mainstay of long-nosed and long-footed potoroos and of Tasmanian and brush-tailed bettongs. In relatively cool areas where fungi are most abundant, they can comprise as much as 80 percent of an animal's diet.

Most of the fungi utilized by rat kangaroos are not the familiar mushroom types, but ones that produce their small, globular fruiting bodies beneath the surface. The long-nosed potoroo eats around fifty varieties of these fungi, which grow in association with tree roots, enhancing their nutrient uptake. Because the fungi rely on fungivorous animals to spread their spores, there is a complex relationship between the abundance of potoroos, the dispersal of fungi, and the maintenance of healthy trees.

One problem with this diet is that fungi do not contain the right balance of essential amino acids needed by their consumers. But studies of the brush-tailed bettong have shown that the animals can correct this imbalance by the process of prolonged fermentation of food in the forechamber of the stomach. The microbes that carry out this fermentation change the composition of the broth, giving it a more appropriate nutritional balance. ■

Dave Watts/ANT/NHPA

INSECTS

are an important source of protein for the musk rat kangaroo (below). *Gripping its prey tightly, it cracks open the tough insect casing with its bladelike premolar teeth.*

Illustration Stephen Message/Wildlife Art Agency

LIFE CYCLE

Once a female rat kangaroo reaches sexual maturity, at about one year of age, reproduction becomes an almost constant part of her life. With just a few exceptions, such as the musk rat kangaroo and some populations of the burrowing bettong, breeding is nonseasonal and females can breed at any time of the year. Moreover, the phenomenon of embryonic diapause (see right) means that as soon as a female's pouch becomes empty another birth is already approaching. Not surprisingly, rat kangaroos tend to produce more than one offspring a year, and a female brush-tailed bettong, starting in some cases as early as six months of age, may give birth to three consecutive young per year for several years of reproductive life.

Male rat kangaroos tend to reach maturity shortly after their female counterparts and invest much less time and energy in producing offspring. By visiting females neighboring his home range, a male finds out which are coming into estrus and, unless driven off, lingers nearby until potential partners are ready to mate. Usually courtship approaches are simple, although musk rat kangaroos may court for several days, facing each other standing upright and gently pawing each other's head and neck.

inSIGHT

DIAPAUSE

In most kangaroos, a process of delayed birth, known as embryonic diapause, can take place. Female rat kangaroos often mate soon after the birth of an offspring—in some cases on the same night. Should the resulting embryo develop as normal it would be born before the pouch is vacated and ready for it. Instead, its development is delayed; the embryo is held in limbo and its growth is not resumed until the pouch is empty. This overlap between offspring ensures the mother can breed rapidly: In the Tasmanian bettong, a female may give birth on the same night as her previous young ends its pouch life. Should the first offspring perish, the delayed embryo will resume development at once.

RAT KANGAROOS
are energetic breeders. Having found a female nearing receptivity, the male follows her persistently until she is prepared to mate (above right). If she is not ready for him, she growls, rolls over, and lashes out at him.

GROWING UP
The life of a young honey possum

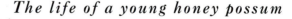

THE NEWLY EMERGED YOUNG
are soon able to ride around on their mother's back as she forages (below). A full litter is too much for her to bear for long, however, and shortly before they are weaned the young follow her on foot.

HONEY POSSUMS
are mature at about six months of age, and adults (above) may mate in any month of the year, although the lack of food in summer means that births are few at that time of year.

UP TO FOUR YOUNG
are born in each litter and all of them may find their way to the pouch; they are the smallest newborn young of any mammal. As they suckle (right), they increase five times in weight before leaving the pouch at about two months of age.

GROWING UP
The life of a rufous rat kangaroo

FAST BREEDER

The female gives birth to her tiny, embryonic offspring, which crawls through her body fur from the birth canal to the pouch (right). Within hours, she is ready to mate again.

THE YOUNG RAT KANGAROO

clings steadfastly to a teat for its first two months, but within four months of birth it has left the pouch for good. Its mother will send it off to cope for itself when her next offspring develops (below).

For the first few weeks of life, young rufous rat kangaroos seek the shelter of the nursery nest, and their mother returns periodically to suckle them (below).

The minuscule, grublike young, about 0.6 in (15 mm) in length, attaches itself to one of four teats in the pouch and grows fast, nourished on its mother's milk. As early as seven or eight weeks it is ready to release the teat and soon starts to make its first trips outside the pouch. Pouch life finally ends at three to four and a half months.

In the Tasmanian bettong, the last two weeks of pouch life are characterized by ever shorter stays in this "mobile home," until a stage is reached when the young seeks its safety only when startled. A few nights later, the mother's pouch muscles dramatically tighten and the youngster is forcibly and permanently evicted, although the mother continues to suckle the offspring for several more weeks until weaning is complete. ∎

After mating, all the hard work is left up to the female. Following a gestation period ranging from twenty-one days in bettongs to thirty-eight days in the long-nosed potoroo—one of the longest gestations for a marsupial—a single young is born. Twins are usual in the musk rat kangaroo, but in all other species if two young emerge only one will survive in the pouch.

FROM BIRTH TO DEATH

RUFOUS RAT KANGAROO	MUSK RAT KANGAROO
BREEDING: THROUGHOUT THE YEAR	**BREEDING:** FEBRUARY–JULY
GESTATION: 22–24 DAYS	**GESTATION:** NOT KNOWN
LITTER SIZE: USUALLY 1	**LITTER SIZE:** 2 OR 3
NO. OF LITTERS: UP TO 3 PER YEAR	**NO. OF LITTERS:** ONE PER YEAR
WEIGHT AT BIRTH: LESS THAN 0.03 OZ (1 G)	**WEIGHT AT BIRTH:** LESS THAN 0.03 OZ (1 G)
LEAVES POUCH: 16 WEEKS	**LEAVES POUCH:** 21 WEEKS
WEANING: 22 WEEKS	**WEANING:** 22–23 WEEKS
SEXUAL MATURITY: 11–13 MONTHS	**SEXUAL MATURITY:** 12 MONTHS
LONGEVITY: 6 YEARS OR MORE	**LONGEVITY:** NOT KNOWN

Illustrations Carol Roberts

R. J. Allingham/ANT/NHPA

TALES OF DECLINE

IN A CONTINENT WITH MORE THAN ITS FAIR SHARE OF RARE SPECIES, FEW MAMMAL FAMILIES CAN RIVAL THE TRAGIC RECORD OF DECLINE THAT HAS BESET THE RAT KANGAROOS OVER THE LAST TWO CENTURIES

The modern-day story of Australia's rat kangaroo family makes depressing reading. Many marsupials in the continent have suffered drastic cuts in their ranges and populations since European colonization set in motion large-scale changes to Australia's natural environment. But for the rat kangaroos the outcome seems particularly harsh because almost every species in the family has suffered severe decline or is under threat. Two are almost certainly now extinct and two more have crashed from widespread abundance to distributions less than one percent the size of their historic ranges. Of the others, three have vanished from wide sections of their former ranges and three are confined to limited areas.

It is likely that some rat kangaroos, such as the long-nosed potoroo, were already contracting in range by the time Europeans began settling in Australia from the late 18th century. But the downfalls that came after colonization certainly eclipsed any natural declines. The survival pressures exerted on rat kangaroos were, and are, both indirect and direct. Of the first type are crucial alterations to the abundance and composition of the plant life on which the animals depend: changes brought about by the grazing of introduced livestock and rabbits, by the spread of exotic plants, and by new patterns of bushfire. Of the second type are direct reductions in rat kangaroo numbers caused by destruction of habitat and predation by introduced foxes and cats.

BELEAGUERED BETTONGS

Among the rat kangaroos, the bettongs have suffered most dramatically. In the early decades of European colonization, the brush-tailed bettong was familiar throughout the south, from the coast of Western Australia to the Dividing Range in New South Wales; it was still common in South Australia at the turn of the century. Yet by the early 1980s it

survived only in three pockets of woodland in the southwestern corner of the continent. Its decline resulted mainly from the removal of vital shrub cover by agricultural clearance, grazing, and fire.

Controlled fires lit by settlers tended to be less intense but more frequent than the natural fires that raged periodically in the bush; though they burned undergrowth, they produced too little heat to germinate buried seeds and left insufficient time for plant cover to regenerate. As the cover thinned, the animals were more vulnerable to predators, especially to their newfound enemy, the fox.

The burrowing bettong has endured an even more drastic decline. It faced a battery of pressures on the mainland, including vegetation removal by farmers, sheep, and rabbits; hunting by cats and

Although confined to coastal northeastern Queensland, the musk rat kangaroo still survives in good numbers.

Dave B. Fleetham/Natural Science Photos

Jean-Paul Ferrero/Ardea

This map shows the former and current distribution of the burrowing bettong.

///// **FORMER**   ▮ **CURRENT**

Early explorers found the burrowing bettong one of the most abundant animals in the Australian interior, and its burrow systems, now occupied by rabbits, can still be seen in the outback. The bettong's decline began early, and it finally died out on the mainland in the 1940s. Today about 5,000 burrowing bettongs remain—on Barrow Island off the Pilbara coast, as well as on Bernier and Dorre Islands in Shark Bay.

foxes; and poisoning by farmers who considered the animal a pest. Similar pressures also killed off the last Tasmanian bettongs from the mainland over sixty years ago, and, though they remain in fairly healthy numbers overall, the survivors in Tasmania are continually being pushed from former habitats by the conversion of land to intensive pasture or arable farming. Heavy grazing not only destroys vegetation cover for the animals, it also makes underground fungi less abundant and harder to dig out because the soil is compacted by trampling.

The fourth of this genus, the northern bettong, is so rare and restricted in range that it remains little known. As far as is known, it lives only in the Davies Creek area of northern Queensland, and should foxes reach this site it could quickly vanish.

Once widespread across Australia, the burrowing bettong survives today on only three islands.

ALONGSIDE MAN

BOUNTY HUNTERS

Humans have generally meant bad news for rat kangaroos through their impact on habitats and introduction of cats and dogs. Burrowing bettongs were once also poisoned as pests, as some Tasmanian bettongs are today. In 1892, during a time when bounties were paid on almost any hopping marsupial, some 80,000 rufous rat kangaroos and bettongs succumbed in one district of New South Wales alone.

However, bounty hunting probably had little impact on overall numbers. The same applies to past traditional hunting of the desert rat kangaroo. Yalliyanda Aborigines caught it for food simply by sneaking up on its nest in the daytime, closing the escape hole, and grabbing the occupant by hand.

ANT/NHPA

The rufous rat kangaroo, by contrast, is one of the best-known rat kangaroos of eastern Australia and can coexist with livestock as long as some cover remains. Wood clearance has, however, pushed it from many areas, and foxes may have caused its demise in large southern sections of its former range.

Like the rufous rat kangaroo, the long-nosed potoroo still has a reasonably extensive distribution, but because the animal depends on dense vegetation, it is vulnerable wherever burning and other land-clearance operations are practiced. Its former

Recently discovered, the long-footed potoroo is probably doomed to extinction unless its existing forest habitat is preserved.

population in southwestern Australia died out earlier this century, and it no longer survives in South Australia. Elsewhere, habitat modification and destruction have tended to fragment the suitable patches of habitat within its range. Records of the long-footed potoroo, on the other hand, have only ever come from a very limited area. Rare and little studied, this species was only described to science as late as 1980. Logging is scheduled to take place in forests near some of the few sites where it has been recorded, raising fears for its survival.

ILL-FATED POTOROOS

The fate of the broad-faced potoroo has long been sealed. The first of the rat kangaroos to die out after colonization, this species was last taken from the wild in 1875. Already confined to open tracts in the southwest of the continent, it was in steady decline by the time settlers hastened its demise. The desert rat kangaroo has not been seen since 1935; like the broad-faced potoroo, it occupied a small range and was probably never abundant in its habitat. Though hopes are held out that a small population may still survive somewhere in the inhospitable Lake Eyre Basin, the chances must be considered slim.

The musk rat kangaroo still exists in healthy numbers in the pockets of rain forest along the north Queensland coast—but in those tracts where trees have been cleared for agricultural development, the species has disappeared. Like most rain-forest creatures, it simply cannot survive outside its uniquely rich, closed-canopy environment. ■

RAT KANGAROOS IN DANGER

NO FEWER THAN HALF OF THE EIGHT SURVIVING SPECIES OF RAT KANGAROOS ARE CLASSED AS IN DANGER OF EXTINCTION UNLESS STRINGENT CONSERVATION MEASURES GIVE THEM A FIGHTING CHANCE TO RECOVER:

BRUSH-TAILED BETTONG	ENDANGERED
BURROWING BETTONG	ENDANGERED
NORTHERN BETTONG	ENDANGERED
LONG-FOOTED POTOROO	ENDANGERED

ENDANGERED MEANS THAT THE ANIMAL IS IN DANGER OF EXTINCTION AND ITS SURVIVAL IS UNLIKELY UNLESS STEPS ARE TAKEN TO SAVE IT.

INTO THE FUTURE

Preserving those populations of rat kangaroos that still remain, and perhaps giving some the prospect of increasing in number, are great challenges for conservationists in Australia. Some progress has already been made, while other measures will become increasingly necessary in the future.

Laws controlling the killing of these animals are already well advanced—the rufous rat kangaroo is protected, for example, even in the states where it is widespread—but legislation alone is not always effective. Raising public awareness of the vulnerability of the Tasmanian bettong, for instance, is vital if the use of poison is to be limited. Perhaps of more importance is legislation against the removal of natural vegetation, since habitat loss is a more serious cause of decline than direct persecution.

Protection of habitats on commercially owned land would augment the system of preserves and

PREDICTION

STAVING OFF EXTINCTION

Though the adverse threats to rat kangaroos as a whole are unlikely to abate, there is hope that careful conservation efforts, combined with public-awareness campaigns, can enable the populations of some of the most endangered species to recover to the extent that extinction no longer looms on the horizon.

sanctuaries set up in Australia specifically to protect habitats and their wildlife. The woodland and island refuges of the brush-tailed and burrowing bettongs are already wildlife preserves, and the northern bettong's home lies within the Davies Creek National Park.

Preserves can be managed to enhance their suitability for wildlife. Because fire can open up ground cover and may stimulate the fruiting of fungi, controlled burning could benefit some rat kangaroos; it has already been tried for the brush-tailed bettong. Though fires must be hot enough to promote seed germination, their spread must be checked enough to leave patches of intact shelter vegetation.

Another way forward lies in the control of alien predators, especially foxes. Poison-baiting of meat is effective against foxes without harming native wildlife, and has been one of the key factors behind a recent increase in the population of brush-tailed bettongs in the Dryandra Woodland. ∎

BOUNCING BACK

In 1992, several decades after the species' disappearance from mainland Australia, the burrowing bettong made its first comeback. A group of the animals was transferred from Dorre Island to a long, narrow peninsula known as Heirisson Prong, pointing out from the mainland into Shark Bay. A 3,000-acre (1,200-ha) section of the peninsula has been closed off with a fence, and beyond that a 12.5-mile- (20-km-) wide belt of land is being poison-baited in an attempt to create a fox-free and cat-free refuge for the bettongs. The rapid progress of this reintroduction—within five months of release the colony had increased its numbers by 50 percent—has encouraged plans for further releases in the Gibson Desert region and in South Australia.

ISLAND REFUGE

Concern that the brush-tailed bettong was on the verge of extinction provoked conservationists to take the drastic step of transferring forty animals to the secure, predator-free St. Francis Island off South Australia in 1981. Since then, however, the population in the preserves has fared well—so much so that reintroductions from the wild stock have started to take place in carefully protected mainland sites where the species formerly ranged. Reintroduction may also be possible using captive-bred animals.

Illustration Kim Thompson

NEW WORLD RATS & MICE

RELATIONS

The New World rats and mice are members of the enormous Muridae family within the rodent order. Other murids include:

LEMMINGS

HAMSTERS

GERBILS

JIRDS

Michael Fogden/Oxford Scientific Films

NEW WORLD HORDES

FROM THE CHILL CANADIAN FORESTS TO THE ROCKY TIP OF PATAGONIA—EVEN ON REMOTE OCEANIC ISLANDS—THE AMERICAS ARE CRAWLING WITH RATS AND MICE IN IMMEASURABLE NUMBERS

ORDER

Rodentia
(rodents)

FAMILY

Muridae
(rats, mice, and
their allies)

SUBFAMILY

Hesperomyinae
(New World rats
and mice)

GENERA

about 70

SPECIES

about 370

little boy opens the door of his log cabin, eager to show his parents some cactus blossoms he had collected from the desert floor. But instead of finding his colorful souvenirs, all he can see is a neat pile of dull gray pebbles. There are no fresh footprints or tire tracks. There had been no noise during the night, apart from the distant howls of coyotes. The disappearance of the blossoms—and their drab replacements—remains a mystery.

Newcomers to the American Southwest might never solve the mystery of the missing blossoms. But a local would offer a simple solution: pack rat. Several species of North American wood rats have earned that title because of their impulse to hoard, and sometimes to trade, bright, colorful objects.

Pack rats thrive in the hot, desertified lands of the southwestern United States and northern Mexico. They are members of a larger group of rodents—in fact, the largest single group of mammals—called the

in SIGHT

PARALLEL LINES

Many species of New World rats and mice, seemingly unique in their ecological niche, actually mirror similar Old World species. The deer mouse closely resembles the European long-tailed field mouse. Likewise, harvest mice in the two hemispheres seem like close relatives, and the water rat of southern Brazil resembles the common rat.

Such parallel development of unrelated lineages is called convergent evolution. The drying out of land some 28 million years ago created new grasslands, which the New World rats and mice quickly colonized. More than 20 million years later, South America proved to be a literal breeding ground for yet more diversification that mirrored evolution in Europe, Africa, and Asia. The new land bridge ushered in North American hesperomids, which settled into niches unoccupied by other rodents.

New World rats and mice, represented almost throughout the Americas. Overall there are some 370 species of these rodents, usually grouped as the subfamily Hesperomyinae (hes-per-o-MIE-in-ie). The principal difference between hesperomids and their Old World counterparts of the subfamily Murinae is slight: New World rats and mice lack a row of projections inside their upper molars.

A subfamily as wide-ranging as the hesperomids would be expected to exhibit a range of body types. Many species do just that, with unique adaptations to, for example, the Sonoran Desert of the Southwest, the humid forests of equatorial South America, and the oxygen-starved slopes of the high Andes.

A much greater number of hesperomids, however, have adjusted to a wider range of habitats and can be described as generalists. The deer mouse is the best example. With nearly fifty species spread over the Americas, it epitomizes the success of the subfamily as a whole. It has few specialist adaptations to the normal mouse anatomy, and individual deer mouse species differ only in their coloration, which corresponds with their surroundings.

HESPEROMID HISTORY

The first New World species lived in forests, but recognizably hesperomid rats and mice evolved as climatic changes pulled back the forest cover and

A pair of white-footed mice, also known as deer mice, forage upon a sprig of wild cherry.

K. Maslowski/Frank Lane Picture Agency

widened the range of habitats. The greatest diversification of the subfamily occurred five million years ago, when hesperomids poured through the new land gateway into South America.

South America had very little contact with other continents at that time. One of the many odd results of this isolation was the absence of rodents. Hesperomids soon filled the vacuum, initially developing adaptations for the vast open grasslands. Most of the continent also lacked insectivorous mammals or members of the order Lagomorpha—the rabbits, hares, and pikas. There again, the rats and mice proved to be adaptable. Hesperomids such as mole mice, shrew mice, and rabbit rats filled the ecological niches occupied by moles, shrews, and rabbits on other continents. Other species floated to islands in the Caribbean and off the western coast of South America, where they split into separate genera.

If the deer mouse of North America provides the basic prototype of the subfamily, then the South

Some of the newest hesperomid discoveries include spiny rats (above) *from South American forests.*

Haraldo Palo Jr./NHPA

American species are the "limited edition" specialists of Hesperomyinae. The radiation of species within South America accounts for the most dramatic adaptations among the New World rats and mice.

Tree-dwellers, such as the Central American climbing rats, have long tails and broad feet adapted to climbing. Some burrowing species, such as the Brazilian shrew mouse, have extremely short tails, greatly reduced eyes, and a cone-shaped snout that suits a burrowing lifestyle.

The puna mouse, which lives on windswept plains at altitudes of up to 17,000 feet (5,200 m), has adapted to its barren habitat in a number of ways. Its stocky build and long fur offer protection from the intense cold, and its complex set of molars allow it to gnaw the sparse Andean vegetation. Like many of the most specialized New World rats and mice, the puna mouse constitutes a single-species genus— *Punomys*. In contrast, generalist genera such as *Peromyscus* (deer mice), *Oryzomys* (rice rats), and *Akodon* (South American field mice) all contain dozens of species.

In concentrating on all the variations within the Hesperomyidae, it is too easy to overlook the many shared characteristics within the subfamily. One is size. With only a few exceptions, New World rats and mice are small, and most are nocturnal. Another link is life span, which in turn is linked to breeding patterns. Few of these animals live more than a year or two in the wild. They breed early and often, making up in fecundity what they lack in longevity. ■

ⒶNCESTORS

THE MISSING LINK

Some zoologists link the New World rats and mice with hamsters. It seems certain that the primitive ancestors of the hesperomids were the cricetid rodents, which lived in North America about 33 million years ago. These cricetids had developed about five million years earlier in the Old World and are now seen as the ancestors of hamsters in Europe and Asia and the pouched rats in Africa.

Fossil records indicate that there was a shared Old and New World evolution into the mid-Miocene era, some 25 million years ago, when members of the genus *Copemys* migrated from Eurasia into North America. The link seems to end there, as there are no more recent examples of such generic matches.

Color illustrations Evi Antoniou

PYGMY MICE
Baiomyini
(*bie-o-mie-EE-nee*)

The pygmy mice and brown mice form one of four North American tribes traditionally grouped together. Members of this aggregation range from northern Canada as far south as Panama. The other three tribes are the wood rats, deer mice, and Central American climbing rats.

BURROWING MICE
Oxymycterus
(*ox-ee-MICK-teh-rus*)

The nine species of burrowing mice range across most of tropical South America. They, along with the related genera of Andean rats, shrew mice, mole mice, and Mount Roraima mice, make up the Oxymycterini tribe.

RICE RATS
Oryzomyini
(*o-riz-o-MIE-ee-nee*)

The twenty-five species of Paramo rats (or mice) are grouped within the genus Thomasomys, largely because of their distribution along the forested slopes of the eastern Andes. Together with three other genera they form the tribe Thomasomyini. This group also includes the rice rats (left) and their relatives.

DORMICE

JUMPING MICE AND BIRCH MICE

THE HESPEROMIDS' FAMILY TREE

All rats and mice are murids—members of the Muridae (MEW-rid-ie) family of rodents. The New World rats and mice form the Hesperomyinae (hes-per-o-MIE-in-ie) subfamily of murids; there are fifteen other murid subfamilies. Scientists often range the hesperomids under six main groups.

LEAF-EARED MICE
Phyllotini
(fill-o-TEE-nee)

The eight species of cotton rats, genus Sigmodon, range across the southern United States, Mexico, Central America, and a northern swath of South America. Marsh rats, genus Holochilus, **with four species, join them to form the Sigmodontini tribe. Other tribes in this group are the leaf-eared mice (right) and their relatives, and the southern water rats and their relatives.**

FISH-EATING RAT
Ichthyomyini
(ik-thee-o-mie-EE-nee)

A single tribe comprises and gives its name to this group of New World rats and mice. There are three genera, ranging across the foothills and Andean mountains of equatorial South America: fish-eating rats, water mice, and the single species of Ecuadorian fish-eating rat.

VESPER RAT
Nyctomys sumichrasti
(nick-TO-miss soo-mee-CRASS-tee)

Two arboreal species, the vesper rat of Central America and the Yucatan vesper rat, make up the single tribe Nictomyini in this group. Both species are highly adapted to life high in the trees—typified by the clawed big toes on the hind feet.

JERBOA

OTHER RATS AND MICE (MURIDAE)

ALL RODENTS

B/W illustrations Ruth Grewcock

ANATOMY:
THE DEER MOUSE

New World rats and mice range in size from the pygmy mouse, which can measure less than 3.5 in (90 mm) from nose to tail, to the South American giant rat (above left), which can reach 18 in (45 cm) in total length. (House mouse is pictured for comparison.)

THE EYES

are prominent in most deer mice. This enables them to see better at night.

THE NOSE

is acutely pointed, owing to the nasal bones of the skull, which project beyond the upper incisors. Like most rodents, the deer mouse has a highly developed sense of smell.

THE FEET

have claws on all digits, as in most hesperomids. There is great variation among hesperomid species, however. Some burrowing species have much more developed claws, whereas marsh rats and other semiaquatic species have webbed feet.

FOREFOOT

SKELETON

The basic mouselike anatomy of the deer mouse is unspecialized, a reflection of its generalized range of habitats and feeding patterns. In fact, it closely resembles the anatomy of the European long-tailed field mouse. The tail is shorter than the length of the head and body combined, except in tree-dwelling species.

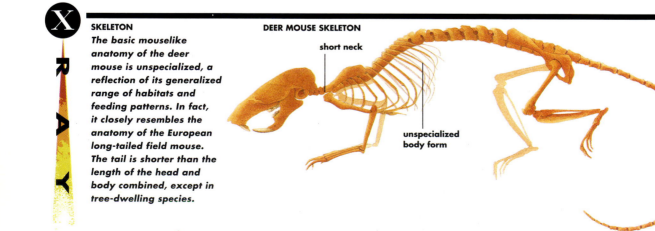

DEER MOUSE SKELETON

short neck

unspecialized body form

X

R A Y

X-ray illustrations Elisabeth Smith

THE EARS

provide extremely keen hearing, which is often used defensively. In common with many hesperomid species, deer mice also emit high-pitched squeaks as a territorial marking device or in alarm.

SPINY RICE RAT

Named after their bristly coats, these rats feed at night on seeds. Many island species are now close to extinction.

VESPER RAT

This long-tailed Central American species is an excellent climber. It nests in trees, where it feeds on fruit.

SOUTH AMERICAN FIELD MOUSE

These mice forage on the ground for insects, as well as fruit, seeds, and green plant matter. Some of them also burrow well.

CENTRAL AMERICAN WATER MOUSE

Equipped with webbed hind feet, water mice live in mountain streams, where they feed on snails and, perhaps, fish.

THE SOFT FUR

varies greatly in color among deer mice according to where they live. Those inhabiting temperate forests are usually camouflaged with a grayish-brown upper fur, whereas those living in more open terrain have a paler coloration.

FACT FILE:

THE DEER MOUSE

CLASSIFICATION

GENUS: *PEROMYSCUS*

SPECIES: *MANICULATUS*

SIZE

HEAD-BODY LENGTH: 2.8–6.7 IN (70–170 MM)

TAIL LENGTH: 1.6–8 IN (40–205 MM)

WEIGHT: 0.5–3.2 OZ (15–90 G)

WEIGHT AT BIRTH: 0.1 OZ (2.3 G)

COLORATION

GRAY OR SANDY TO GOLDEN OR DARK BROWN ON THE BACK AND UPPER PARTS; WHITE OR OFF-WHITE ON THE UNDERPARTS AND FEET SOME SPECIES ARE NEARLY ALL WHITE; OTHERS ARE NEARLY ALL BLACK

FEATURES

SPARSELY HAIRED TAIL IS AT LEAST ONE-THIRD OF TOTAL LENGTH; EYES AND EARS ARE LARGE IN RELATION TO BODY

THE TAIL

has only a thin coating of hair, like that of a house mouse or a wood mouse. Some deer mice can let the tip of the tail slip off the vertebrae as a way of escaping predators.

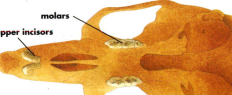

SKULL

The brain-to-body-weight ratio varies among deer mice species and is linked to habitat. Those facing upheavals of climate or food supply have smaller brains. Those in stable

MEXICAN DEER MOUSE SKULL

molars

upper incisors

TEETH

Unlike Old World rats and mice, hesperomids have no rounded projections on the inner side of the upper molars. The teeth of some insect-eating hesperomids are greatly reduced—particularly molars.

habitats have larger brains, a trend that is linked to their increased longevity and smaller litter size. Burrowing species have thinner, more conical skulls and deeper eye sockets.

lower incisors

cheek arch

NICHE SPECIALISTS

NEW WORLD RATS AND MICE OWE MUCH OF THEIR SUCCESS TO THEIR ABILITY TO DIVERSIFY, ADAPTING IN FORM AND LIFESTYLE IN ORDER TO EXPLOIT EVEN THE TINIEST OF HABITATS

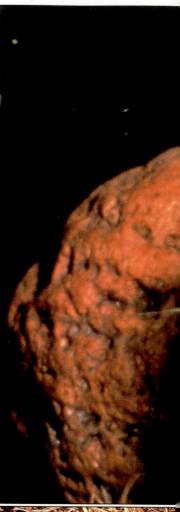

The main feature of New World rats and mice is their adaptability, which is partly explained by their abundant stock of genetic material. Indeed, the ultimate proof of species and subspecies diversity within the subfamily lies in the study of the structure and function of cell nuclei.

The subfamily was initially subdivided along the easiest points of reference, such as physical form and adaptation to habitat. The numerous hesperomid genera and species are grouped into thirteen hesperomid tribes, which themselves can be merged into a classification of six groups (see Family Tree, page 1878). These looser classifications concentrate more on habitat than on some of the less obvious variations such as in teeth and chromosomes.

More recently, however, particularly in the last 30 years, cell studies have identified key chromosomal differences among genera and even within some species—and the amount of chromosomal material to identify is stupendous. The Chibchan water mouse of Venezuela, for example, has 92 paired chromosomes, the highest number in any mammal.

Adaptability is also a handy word with which to generalize about a subfamily numbering at least 370 species. These rats and mice thrive in most habitats, from deserts to humid tropical forests. Moreover, they are often abundant within these habitats, strengthening their position as primary consumers in a number of complex food chains.

SUBTLE VARIETY

Hesperomid variations, however, occur within a narrow size range. No living species exceeds 12 in (30 cm) in head-and-body length, although some extinct species were much larger. It has been argued that the very size of these species worked against their survival when they first encountered European mammalian predators and Old World rats and mice—

particularly the *Rattus* genus containing the black, or common, and brown, or Norwegian, rats. Until the arrival of Europeans—human or otherwise—the New World species had few defensive instincts.

The smaller species were more able to radiate into the ecological niches that now typify the variation within the Hesperomyidae subfamily. They now encompass most lifestyles: terrestrial (ground-based), arboreal (living in trees), fossorial (burrowing), and semiaquatic (swimming).

The terrestrial species, including deer mice, rice rats, and harvest mice, are the most numerous. They conform most to the typical mouselike anatomy, with

M. P. L. Fogden/Bruce Coleman Ltd.

S. Roberts/Ardea

The bushy-tailed wood rat (above) is one of the pack rats, famed for their hoarding traits.

MOUSE GUILDS

There are about fifty species of deer mice, with a range extending from northern Canada south to the Isthmus of Panama. It is not uncommon for several deer mouse species to overlap in distributional range. The mice respond to this habitat overlap by observing a type of segregation. Such an arrangement, known as a guild, is based on the relative size of each species.

Size determines the feeding pattern and the fecundity of a species. Within a three-species guild, for example, the largest species would have the most specific requirements for food—perhaps large seeds and nuts—as well as for nesting sites. Smaller species become progressively more wide-ranging in their foraging and more adaptable about where to build their nests.

a tail that is shorter than the combined head-and-body length. By contrast, some arboreal species, such as the American climbing mouse, have markedly longer tails to act as counterbalances when they jump from one tree to the next. Fossorial species, such as the shrew mouse and mole mouse, have almost vestigial tails to facilitate life in tunnels and chambers; other adaptations to burrowing include narrow skulls and lengthened claws.

The four species of fish-eating or aquatic rats of Central and South America, as well as the Central American water mice, have some profound adaptations. The rats are about the size of common rats of the genus *Rattus*, but the head and body are flattened, eyes and ears are small, and the broad hind feet are partially webbed. The Central American water mice are even more adapted to an aquatic lifestyle. Nostrils open backward and are protected by flaps, and the streamlined body means that the forelimbs hardly project. Webbed hind feet and a flared tail propel these mice through rapid tropical streams. The glossy outer fur and dense underfur also indicate adaptation to a watery lifestyle.

The vast majority of New World rats and mice are nocturnal, owing to their small size and the abundance of diurnal predators in most habitats. The day-active exceptions are mainly native to the high Andes or other regions where the overall animal population is low. ■

A grasshopper mouse delivers a loud, piercing call upon discovering another mouse nearby.

HABITATS

Consider a detailed map of North, Central, and South America in order to imagine the range of habitats occupied by New World rats and mice. Remember that these rodents have successfully colonized the entire landmass except for the very coldest regions of northern Alaska and Canada and the snowiest ridges of the Rockies and Andes.

The map exercise succeeds in conveying the sense of scale of their range, but more important it should show where—and why—certain members of the subfamily were forced to specialize or adapt. Working from north to south, one can visualize the broad swaths of North American forest or prairie. Below them are the arid deserts of the American Southwest and northern Mexico, followed by Central American rain forests that extend into the Amazon Basin of South America. Rounding off this Cook's tour of New World geography are the pampas (grassy plains) of temperate South America and finally dry, windswept Patagonia.

These descriptions paint a broad-brush view of the landscapes of the Americas. They also emphasize the scope of these habitats. Imagine regions the size of western Europe with similar climate and plant life. It is not surprising that a mammal, having succeeded in one part of such a region, should do so across its full extent. The hesperomid subfamily is just such an example. Its exact origins in North America are obscure; perhaps its ancestors swept across the Bering Strait from Asia millions of years ago, just as the Amerindians did about twelve thousand years ago. The generalist species of North America show how these rodents could occupy these macrohabitats.

WIDE-RANGING COLONISTS

The fifty or so species of deer mice range from Canada to Mexico, with some individual species—such as *Peromyscus maniculatus*—occupying that full range. These agile animals are at home on grassland and in scrub, as well as in their original forest habitat. No other North American hesperomids can match the vast range of deer mice, but there are other noteworthy generalists, such as the nineteen species of harvest mice that thrive throughout the west and south of the continent. As their name suggests, they are most at home in grasslands and near crop fields, but many species do well in forest, desert, and even tropical environments.

Likewise, the nineteen species of wood rats feature in most environments of the western United States, Mexico, and Central America. They include

The gray bushy-tailed wood rat (below) *ranges south to the Dakotas and Arizona.*

Gary R. Jones/Ardea

Hesperomids live almost everywhere in the New World, from parts of Alaska to Patagonia. They are absent only from the coldest regions—the northernmost edge of North America and the snow-capped peaks of the Rockies and Andes. Generalist species such as the deer mouse occupy large ranges, but there are many specialist species that thrive in strictly defined territories marked off by climate or landscape. Some island species, both in the Caribbean and on Pacific islands such as the Galápagos, have been unable to tolerate the arrival of humans and the common rats that accompanied them.

DISTRIBUTION

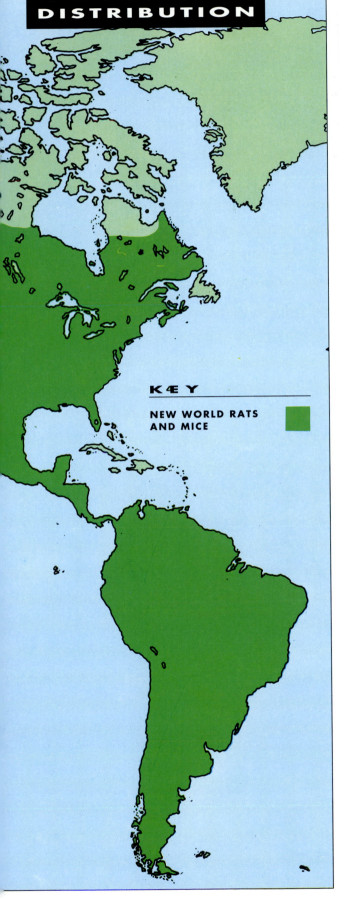

KEY

NEW WORLD RATS AND MICE ▮

The climbing mice of Central and South America are tiny but nimble inhabitants of moist, tropical gallery forest (above).

the famous pack rats, which amuse and sometimes infuriate humans with their kleptomania.

Rice rats, with fifty-seven species, are the largest single group of New World rats and mice. They are also true internationalists, with a range that extends from the southern United States, through Central America and into Bolivia and southern Brazil.

The South American field mice—of which there are up to sixty species—range across nearly all of their continent, making them the Southern Hemisphere equals of the deer mice in their universality. They are active during the day as well as at night, making them somewhat exceptional within the subfamily.

MOVING INTO MICROHABITATS

The same map of America would also show some exceptions to the broad swaths of landscape and climate. The southeastern tip of North America (the present states of Alabama, Georgia, and Florida) was a humid wilderness at the time New World rats and mice radiated across the continents. Some of the

inSIGHT

FOREST TUNNELERS

South America provides hesperomids with a number of ecological niches that are unoccupied by other mammals. The Brazilian shrew mouse has evolved in order to thrive in such niches. It inhabits the highlands in or near the rain forests of eastern Brazil. It spends most of its life underground, burrowing for insects and worms and digging long burrows under the forest litter. Certain adaptations give the shrew mouse an advantage in this sort of life: Its eyes are small and its short ears are covered in fur. The tail is very short, and the clawed forefeet have four functioning digits. The wide hind feet are also clawed. These modifications make the shrew mouse an effective burrower, unlike any other South American mammal. The generic name of the shrew mouse—*Blarinomys*—was inspired by its similarity to the North American short-tailed shrew, *Blarina*.

microhabitats there were confined to a coastal fringe. Up to a dozen deer mouse species and subspecies settled there, adopting specialist adaptations such as sand-colored fur or relying on local plant or insect life for food.

Other specialists emerged from the ranks of the generalists, and there are harvest mice and wood rats now occupying tiny ranges. But the most dramatic adaptations occurred in South America, where the hesperomids penetrated about five million years ago, after the land link opened up from North America. These rats and mice found a much narrower range of mammals and few, if any, other rodents to compete with for food.

A number of single-species genera developed in South America, either in response to microhabitat conditions or to fill an ecological void left through the absence of native insectivores and lagomorphs (rabbits, hares, and pikas). The coney rat is a specialist in the sense that it occupies a rabbitlike niche in the ecosystem. However, it is wide-ranging, extending from northern Uruguay and Chile down to Tierra del Fuego. It inhabits sandy fields, pampas, and cultivated fields—exactly as a rabbit would.

Then there are single-species genera that have specialized in response to landscape. The puna mouse lives in the Peruvian altiplanos (high

plateaus) at altitudes of up to 17,000 feet (5,200 m). Its adaptations—a compact, volelike body. and long, soft fur—are conditioned by the need to survive in its barren, freezing landscape. The altiplano chinchilla mouse also lives in the high Andes, where its dense, soft, and silky fur—so like that of the true chinchilla—keeps it snug. Other hesperomids, including many of the deer mice, experience similar cold occasionally, but none hibernate in the true sense. A deer mouse, for example, will undergo periods of torpor, when its body temperature is reduced for a number of hours or days. ∎

D. Hall/Frank Lane Picture Agency. Inset M. P. L. Fogden/Oxford Scientific Films

FOCUS ON

THE MEXICAN DESERT

Northern Mexico has a mountainous, desert landscape that is a hotter version of its northern neighbors'—the states of Arizona, New Mexico, and Texas. Rainfall is minimal and daytime temperatures often soar past 122°F (50°C), although frosts can sometimes occur at higher altitudes.

The characteristic desert plants are highly adapted to the lack of moisture—yucca trees, various species of cacti, and the agave bush, with its distinctive sword-shaped leaves. Animals must also be hardy to survive in these trying conditions. Many species are nocturnal or spend their lives underground.

Hesperomids fit into this delicate desert food chain. Among them are the three species of grasshopper mice, which thrive in the short-grass prairies and desert scrub. Grasshopper mice feed mainly on grasshoppers, beetles, and other insects. Some even prey on other rodents, including the smaller deer mice.

TEMPERATURE AND RAINFALL

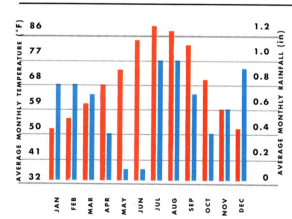

■ TEMPERATURE

■ RAINFALL

The average monthly temperatures and rainfall figures show that the central plateau of northern Mexico fits a typical desert pattern. With the exception of July, spring and summer comprise the driest months of the year.

NEIGHBORS

These deserts support a surprisingly diverse food web, although population densities are low. Herbivores are barely represented, but this is no surprise, given the slim variety of plant species.

KIT FOX

Two species of this small fox are native to the open, sandy areas of western North America.

SCORPION

Although the scorpion's long tail ends in a deadly sting, it is often preyed upon by grasshopper mice.

Neighbor illustrations Joanne Cowne, Carol Roberts

DESERT RANGES

Great coastal ranges dictate the desert climate of northern Mexico. The Sierra Madre Occidental, rising to 10,500 ft (3,200 m), extends down the western flank. In the east are the mountains of the Sierra Madre Oriental, rising to 13,780 ft (4,200 m) or more. Between these ranges lie great basins and a central plateau.

USA

MEXICO

Gulf of Mexico

Sierra Madre Occidental

Sierra Madre Oriental

MEXICO'S MOUNTAINS

BURROWING OWL

The burrowing owl often takes over the abandoned burrows of prairie dogs and other mammals.

SKUNK

The western spotted skunk dens below ground but can climb trees with ease. It eats rodents, birds, and insects.

INDIGO SNAKE

This harmless, peaceable species is the largest snake in the United States, reaching over 9 ft (2.7 m) in length.

TURKEY VULTURE

This most widespread of all New World vultures soars over open country in search of carrion.

GILA MONSTER

The gila monster, the only venomous lizard, lives under rocks. It stores fat reserves in its thick tail.

FOOD AND FEEDING

New World rats and mice display their variety and adaptability in their feeding patterns. As with their lifestyles in general, the subfamily exercises the eating options usually open to mammals: Depending on the species, they eat plants, insects, or fish, and many have an omnivorous diet. Whichever the food choice, hesperomids eat a lot. They must satisfy a high metabolic rate that is their genetic inheritance, along with its other corollaries: a high reproductive rate and short life span. They spend the greater part of their waking hours—the nighttime, for most species—foraging for food.

VERSATILE DEER MICE

The deer mouse is omnivorous, which suits its generalist lifestyle and widespread occurrence. Its diet includes seeds, nuts, fruits, berries, and insects. Sometimes deer mice will even eat carrion, but scavenging is rare. Local areas can become highly populated with several species of deer mice. The mice often respond by adopting a guild system of apportioning food supplies (see page 1883). When a deer mouse spots an insect, such as a beetle or grasshopper, it gives pursuit, snapping at the insect and biting it to death. It will also snap up any slugs in its path, and it devours chafers. These latter larvae can destroy tree roots, and in its insect-killing role the deer mouse is clearly the farmer's friend. It earns less respect, however, through its tendency to raid newly planted crop seeds, which it readily sniffs out. Nevertheless, it is less of an agricultural pest than many other rodent species.

Feeding patterns of a wide-ranging animal such as the deer mouse reflect the relative severity of the seasons. Deer mice in northern parts go about their nocturnal foraging with a particular urgency in the autumn, as they begin storing food for the winter. It is not uncommon for a deer mouse to hoard up to 180 cu in (3,000 cu cm) of food as a winter supply.

Cotton rats have an omnivorous diet. They normally eat plants and small insects, but occasional population booms will reduce the availability of these foods. When such a population explosion occurs, cotton rats will often take quail eggs and chicks, as well as crayfish and fiddler crabs. Similarly, rice rats—normally preferring green vegetation such as reeds and sedges—will eat fish and invertebrates.

Grasshopper mice enjoy what is, probably, the most surprising diet. In addition to eating their own kind from time to time, they are remarkably adept at subduing and eating scorpions, whose plump bodies they crunch up with their pointed molars.

CHANGING TO FIT THE FOOD

South American hesperomid specialists have adapted physiologically to their need for particular foods. The fish-eating rat uses its partially webbed feet for propulsion, but it has other adaptations specifically for feeding. It uses its upper incisor teeth, which are shaped like spikes, to spear fish and drag them ashore.

LATE SNACK

South American climbing rats forage by night. They eat a wide range of foods, including nuts, berries, and leaves (right).

FISH FEAST

A fish-eating rat lives up to its name (below). *These large species feel for aquatic prey with their sensory whiskers.*

THE CRUNCH

Grasshopper mice (below) *live in dry habitats, where they prey heavily on invertebrates.*

(in) S I G H T

INSECTS IN THE SHELL

The thirteen species of burrowing mice that are native to semitropical South America are primarily insectivores, and the digestion of their crunchy prey has had a profound effect upon the way they have adapted through time. The hard insect exoskeleton, or shell, gets much of its strength from a substance called chitin. Similar to the cellulose of plants, chitin is difficult to digest. Insectivores such as burrowing mice must use comparatively large amounts of energy to digest the chitin, producing low amounts of energy as a result. Burrowing mice adjust to these low energy returns by having a low metabolic rate in comparison with other hesperomids. That in turn gives them less reproductive capacity; their litter sizes are rarely larger than two.

Tom McHugh/Oxford Scientific Films

Insectivores, such as the burrowing mice of South America, also show how physical adaptations suit their lifestyle, including eating. Their snouts are narrow, in response to the constant need for burrowing; the narrowness can occur because they have forfeited the use of their molars, which are tiny.

The long claws, used primarily for digging burrows, are also ideal for extracting subterranean arthropods, termites, and larvae.

Even the lack of food or water can produce fascinating adaptations. The highland desert mouse is a specialist of some of the most arid South American landscapes. Its kidneys are extremely efficient at recovering water, and the mouse can exist for long periods without any water intake. Instead it derives its water as a by-product of its own metabolism. ■

VARYING THE MENU

Cotton rats live mainly on vegetation, but, when hungry, they will eat whatever they can find, including crayfish (below) and crabs.

Illustration Priscilla Barrett/Wildlife Art Agency

NESTING

Most New World rats and mice are either nest builders or burrowers. A few species take shelter beneath rocks or take over the nest or burrow of another animal. The wood rats of North America are truly spectacular nest builders. A wood rat den is usually built on the ground, sometimes placed against a rock or tree. It is an elaborate structure, incorporating the shiny detritus accumulated during countless interrupted feeding forays.

Several generations of wood rats will work on a single den until it reaches outstanding proportions—more than 6 ft (up to 2 m) in diameter and height. The nest itself is a cavity measuring about 5–13 in (125–330 mm) in diameter. It is lined with leaves, grass, and shredded bark.

Wood rats in desert regions prefer to build their dens almost exclusively from spiny cactus. With an instinctive ingenuity, these dens are built so that the wood rats can scurry in and out easily, but any predator will be impaled on the cactus.

Eastern wood rats build dens of a similar size, often embellishing them with cans, glass, and feathers. The dens are built of sticks and branches.

The marsh rice rat is an expert swimmer and diver, so it has few qualms about nesting among reeds in wetland habitats (right). Individuals that live on drier soil simply dig burrows.

SPINY DEFENSE

A pack rat brings a sprig of cactus to place at the entrance to its den in the arid deserts of the southwestern United States (below). The spines serve as grisly but effective deterrents to would-be intruders.

Several entrances lead to the two spherical nesting chambers, each about 8 in (20 cm) wide. These wood rats tolerate a number of coinhabitants in their large dens, perhaps as a defensive mechanism. Lizards, snakes, toads, rabbits, and opossums have all been observed in wood rat dens.

Grasshopper mice prefer to burrow in their desert habitat. Sometimes the burrow is inherited from another mammal such as a prairie dog, but usually it is built to specific dimensions: U-shaped, about 20 in (50 cm) long, and 5.5 in (14 cm) below the surface. These mice build similar burrows as escape hatches or simply for seed storage. They are also noted for their characteristic *chip* sound that accompanies confrontations between individuals—usually over territorial limits.

The presence of marsh rice rats is usually betrayed by their distinctive nests, as well as their feeding platforms. Nests are usually made of woven grass and are about 18 in (45 cm) in diameter. They are placed in a slight depression, but sometimes they can be seen more than 3.3 feet (about a meter) above ground level in areas subject to flooding.

Deer mice are much more opportunistic about nest building. Some species live in crevices or under logs. Others build nests in holes in trees, under brush piles, or in deep vegetation. These nests are never built as permanent structures, unlike those of wood rats or grasshopper mice. Throughout much of its range, the common deer mouse builds spherical nests of grass, about 4 in (10 cm) in diameter. Once the nest becomes soiled it is abandoned, so several nests will be built in a single season.

South American field mice, the great generalists of the southern hemisphere, are equally adaptable about nest choice. They will often build globular nests at the end of 16-in (40-cm) burrows, but there is no clear-cut, indisputable pattern about these nests. These field mice are clearly opportunists, and they often prefer to build nests in houses. ■

(in) S I G H T

PACK RATS

In Britain, someone who cannot bear to throw away bits of string, bottle tops, or scrap paper would be described as a "magpie." Americans, who are unfamiliar with the hoarding habits of European magpies, would use the term "pack rat" instead.

This term applies strictly to some of the nineteen species of wood rats, that are native to the western United States and Mexico. They use twigs, foliage, bones, and rocks—indeed, whatever is locally available —to build their dens and houses. Some wood rat houses show the work of several generations of this patchwork building technique.

Wood rats usually find these building materials while they are out foraging. But they are willing to drop these items in favor of anything shiny that they might find on the way back. Campers have often observed these pack rats making off with foil chewing-gum wrappers, cigarette packs, and even small items of silverware. Sometimes these rats leave a pebble in place of something taken, a habit that gives them another nickname: trader rats.

A FIRM FOUNDATION
Some pack rats simply take over a rocky crevice, blocking the gaps with debris (right).

LIFE CYCLE

Nearly every species of the hesperomid subfamily is an example of r selection. This ecological term describes a pattern of breeding and survival in a potentially unstable environment. Animals using successful r selection breed early and often, producing large litters to ensure that at least some of the offspring survive. Within this pattern there are some variations and one or two exceptions, but it serves as a safe generalization about the subfamily as a whole.

The usual hesperomid pattern is for short gestation periods, large litters, early sexual maturity, and short life span. The pygmy mouse is the foremost example of hesperomid r selection. Females can become pregnant when they are only four weeks old, giving birth three weeks later. Climbing rats and cotton rats occupy the other extreme, giving birth to relatively more developed young after a longer gestation period (see Insight below).

Grasshopper mice can breed at any time of year, although they usually do so in late spring and summer. The female is sexually receptive for up to a week at a time, and gestation varies from 26 to 47 days. These mice are spectacularly fecund; the females of one species can produce as many as 12 litters during one breeding season. The youngsters themselves are sexually active within six weeks.

The generalist species conform to the standard pattern, with variations usually ascribed to local climate differences. Those living in environments with extreme climatic fluctuations, such as deer mice in their northern range, produce the greatest numbers of young. Related species living in more stable climates produce fewer—and smaller—litters. Likewise, they live longer and have a larger brain capacity.

REPRODUCTION IN DEER MICE

As in so many areas of hesperomid study, deer mice are the ideal candidates for adding statistical evidence to such broad generalizations. Deer mice in the northern range have a defined breeding period, normally March to October. For those deer mice in milder climates, breeding may also occur throughout the year. Females have a sexually receptive period of between five and seven days; this can sometimes occur immediately after giving birth.

Gestation lasts about twenty-four days (up to forty days in lactating mothers), leading to litters of up to nine, but usually averaging three or four. The newborn deer mice are tiny, weighing just over 0.07 oz (2 g). Their ears unfurl after about three days, but their eyes remain shut for two weeks. Young deer mice remain totally dependent on their mother for another six weeks, although they are usually weaned after about three or four weeks of nursing.

They continue to grow until they are about six months old, but both sexes reach sexual maturity well before that time, and breeding will have begun. This rapid succession of reproductive milestones is necessary for deer mice, which rarely live to two years old in the wild.

Deer mice have proven to be tolerant of other individuals within their territory. Males and females form pairs, but severe weather conditions will often

MATING *takes place above ground, within the security of ground cover* (right).

THE YOUNG *are weaned within a month, but they may not venture from the nest for three or four more weeks. By this time, they are fully furred miniature mice* (right).

---

in SIGHT

MOUSE FACTORIES

The deer mouse and pygmy mouse display a reproductive pattern that typifies that of most New World rats and mice—a short gestation period and a litter of small, hardly developed young.

But there are departures from this norm. The big-eared climbing rat has a gestation period of about fifty days—nearly twice as long as the average—and the newborn rats are fully haired. Their eyes open after about six days—about twice as early as most species. Cotton rats are a mixture of these two patterns, combining a short gestation with well-developed young.

GROWING UP

The life of a young deer mouse

BIRTH

occurs deep underground in a snug nesting chamber lined with dry grass, moss, and feathers. The newborn young are sightless, deaf, and practically naked (above right).

THE YOUNG

are capable of little more than gripping a teat and suckling (above). *Even if the mother moves around in the nest, they will still hang on to their milk supply, trailing along behind her.*

lead to enforced congregations of up to thirteen individuals. In normal conditions, however, most males will define a territory and concentrate on the paired family unit. Confrontations are marked by thin squeaks and sharp buzzings.

Deer mice also drum their forefeet rapidly when excited. This behavior is sometimes related to breeding and territory definition, but most zoologists believe that it is confined to defensive responses to predators. In the same way, some nesting females will warn other females off their territory. ∎

FROM BIRTH TO DEATH

DEER MOUSE

GESTATION: 21–40 DAYS

LITTER SIZE: 1–9, AVERAGE 3–4

BREEDING: MARCH–OCTOBER IN NORTHERN EDGE OF RANGE; NONSEASONAL ELSEWHERE

WEIGHT AT BIRTH: 0.08 oz (2.3 G)

EYES OPEN: 13 DAYS

WEANING: 3–4 WEEKS

FIRST FORAGING: 7–8 WEEKS

SEXUAL MATURITY: 7 WEEKS

LONGEVITY: UP TO 2 YEARS IN THE WILD; UP TO 8 IN CAPTIVITY

PYGMY MOUSE

GESTATION: 20–25 DAYS

LITTER SIZE: 1–5, AVERAGE 2–3

BREEDING: NONSEASONAL IN MOST AREAS

WEIGHT AT BIRTH: 0.04 oz (1.2 G)

EYES OPEN: 10–12 DAYS

WEANING: 14–20 DAYS

FIRST FORAGING: 18–22 DAYS

SEXUAL MATURITY: 28 DAYS IN FEMALE; 70–80 DAYS IN MALE

LONGEVITY: UP TO 3 YEARS IN CAPTIVITY; NOT KNOWN IN WILD

Illustration Joanne Cowne

STRENGTH IN NUMBERS

AMONG THIS HUGE GROUP, FORTUNES ARE INEVITABLY MIXED. WHILE MANY OF THE VERSATILE, FAST-BREEDING MAINLAND SPECIES ARE DOING FINE, THEIR ISLAND COUSINS ARE EITHER EXTINCT OR IN DIRE STRAITS

 The history and evolution of New World rats and mice are good indicators of how, as a whole, they have survived and developed. Originating as a subfamily in North America, they spread and thrived in a wealth of habitats and climatic ranges. They were among the many "winners" in the struggle to hold their own in North America and to colonize South America.

The very linking of North and South America some five million years ago was a natural cataclysm that wiped out many South American marsupial species. Having gained a foothold in South America, the hesperomids prospered through a seesaw of climatic changes that made forest cover expand and recede time and again during the Pleistocene era (3 million to 20,000 years ago). That period echoed the first period of adaptation 15–20 million years before, when the basic tree-dwelling species adapted to the new grasslands.

The ebb and flow of forest cover left many species stranded. Some, no doubt, became extinct. Others, such as the vesper rat of the Central American forests, developed in isolation to become a highly unique New World species. In these areas the Hesperomids were helped by their adaptability and the comparative absence of other rodents.

THE SPREAD OF MANKIND

The greatest threat to the subfamily has been the arrival of mankind, and more specifically European settlement in the Americas. Like the hesperomids, the first humans spread south from North America, having crossed a land bridge from Asia near the end of the last ice age, about 12,000 years ago. These hunters and gatherers made little or no impact on the native rats or mice.

Full-scale European settlement, beginning in the 1500s, had immediate consequences. Ships bringing goods and cargo from Europe also carried murine competitors—the common and brown rats, *Rattus rattus* and *Rattus norvegicus* respectively, and mice such as the house mouse, *Mus musculus*. Records from the English colonies indicate that these European species had colonized most of the east coast of North America by 1680. Hesperomids suddenly found themselves competing with some of the most effective colonists of all mammals.

The next great change was wholesale agricultural clearance, which destroyed much of the temperate forest cover in North America and which continues in the Amazon Basin. The fates of two species of harvest mice of the genus *Reithrodontomys* (reeth-ro-DON-to-miss) typify the mixed fortunes of the subfamily in the face of these clearances.

During the 1800s the western harvest mouse, *Reithrodontomys megalotis*, responded to the clearing of woodlands and long-grass prairies in the

Daphne Kinzler/Frank Lane Picture Agency

Rodents adapt rapidly to human intrusion, especially where food crops are involved (above).

John Shaw/NHPA

This map shows the location of the Galápagos Islands, home of several rare rice rat species.

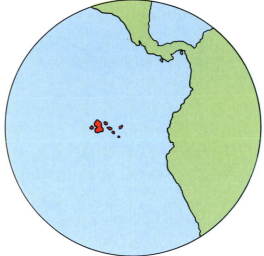

■ GALAPAGOS ISLANDS

Far off the coast of Ecuador, the Galápagos Islands were not discovered until 1535. By then, the indigenous species of rice rats from the genera *Nesoryzomys* and *Oryzomys* had evolved in isolation from any serious competition. Then competition arrived—in the form of rats, dogs, cats, and mongooses— alongside human settlers, who set about cutting down the natural vegetation. Faced with such threats, the rice rats have not fared well. At least five species have died out since the introduction of the black rat.

American Midwest by extending its range considerably. This adaptability echoed the versatility displayed by the harvest mouse's ancestors 25 million years before when the original forest cover rolled back.

The salt marsh harvest mouse, by contrast, faces extinction because of the destruction of its habitat. This mouse is found only in the saltwater and brackish marshes around San Francisco Bay in California. Its remarkable adaptations to this habitat mean that it is one of the few mammals that can drink saltwater. That habitat, like the mouse itself, is endangered by drought, drainage, and industrial growth.

Development—both agricultural and for housing—threatens the Florida mouse, the sole representative of the genus *Podomys*. This ground-dwelling mouse once ranged along the entire length

Friend or foe? Deer mice certainly damage crops, but they also help control agricultural insect pests.

SPECIES

of the Florida peninsula, preferring sand pine scrub and pine oak woodlands. Florida has one of the fastest-growing human populations of any state, and the Florida mouse's preferred habitat is rapidly being replaced by housing developments, citrus groves, and pine plantations. The mouse has virtually disappeared from the Florida coast and is becoming increasingly rare inland.

RATS IN THE GALAPAGOS

Island populations of New World rats and mice face some of the most severe threats. Their resilience and "strength in numbers" are put to the test, sometimes failing after the arrival of humans and, with the humans, the black rat. The Galápagos Islands make a good test ground, where at least seven species of rice rats have been recorded. Some are probably the descendants of individuals that drifted some 625 miles (1,000 km) on rafts of vegetation from the South American mainland, while others may have been introduced by native seafarers many centuries ago.

The islands were used as a base in the 17th and early 18th centuries by English privateers, whose "pirate ships" may well have ferried in the first black rats. Human presence on the Galápagos started in earnest in the last century, when the

---

ALTHOUGH FAR LESS DESTRUCTIVE THAN THE ALIEN BLACK RAT, NATIVE ISLAND RATS HAVE SIMILAR HABITS AND DIETS

---

islands were annexed to mainland Ecuador, and the immigrants—many of whom were, ironically, naturalists—are likely to have brought more rats. Still more rats may have been imported by U.S. military vessels during World War II.

Probably as a direct result of this *Rattus* invasion, the number of indigenous rice rat species has fallen to three. The black rat competes with the local rice rats for food, since it, too, is chiefly a plant-eater. It may also attack and kill the native rats, most of which are smaller. Furthermore, it is suspected of having afflicted some island rats with diseases or parasites against which they would have no defenses. For example, two native species of rice rats were reported as late as 1929 to be thriving on Santa Cruz, an island where there were as yet no black rats. By 1934, however, the rice rats were almost extinct and scientists were finding plentiful specimens of the black rat. For this alien species to have depleted the native rats in so short a time suggests the introduction of a disease, rather than mere competition for food. On Santiago, for example, rice rats survived alongside black rats for nearly three centuries before succumbing.

Ingrid Jeske & Carlo Dani/Natural Science Photos

ENDANGERED

SUN BELT VICTIMS

The United States has seen its human "population center" move steadily south throughout this century. Lower living costs, cheaper heating bills, and an ideal climate for retirement villages have accelerated this trend in the past 20 years. This rapidly growing swath, known as the sun belt, stretches from the Atlantic Coast to the Pacific and covers most of the known habitats of North American hesperomids. Some examples from each coast give an idea of the threats faced by rodents across the range.

The southeastern states of Alabama, Georgia, and Florida have lost vast stretches of coastline in return for higher local tax revenue and improved employment prospects. The threatened coastline includes forests of pine and scrub pine, subtropical bush, and swampy grasslands called everglades. These coastal areas provide the habitat for a number of deer mouse species and subspecies.

Particularly threatened are the pale-coated beach mice, such as the southeastern beach mouse, which figures on the endangered species list compiled by the U.S. Department of the Interior. Their pale coloring, ideal as camouflage on the shore, offers no protection to those that escape to

CONSERVATION MEASURES

● Rats and mice generally make do with the crumbs of conservation causes; the American public has more glamorous rare species to champion. However, the South American hesperomids stand to gain at least generalized environmental awareness. The 1992 Earth Summit, held in Brazil, declared the Amazon rain forest to be a global resource. Any measures taken to protect the forest will clearly work in favor of indigenous rodents.

the more wooded inland regions. Other species, such as the Chadwick Beach cotton mouse of southwestern Florida, may already have disappeared.

The situation 3,100 miles (5,000 km) away on the Pacific Coast is similar. There, the salt marsh harvest mouse and another subspecies native to southern California face a two-pronged threat. Local industrial development and pollution are damaging their delicate habitats, while projects elsewhere in the state are causing irreversible changes to the salt marshes. These threats come from the building of dams and the diversion of inland waterways, which are flushing away the sediment that is needed to feed the ecosystem. Big water projects win votes and create jobs in California, so the outlook looks bleak for these mice.

HESPEROMIDS IN DANGER

THE FOLLOWING SPECIES AND SUBSPECIES ARE A SELECTION OF THOSE LISTED BY THE INTERNATIONAL UNION FOR THE CONSERVATION OF NATURE (IUCN), OR THE WORLD CONSERVATION UNION:

ANTHONY'S WOOD RAT	ENDANGERED
BUNKER'S WOOD RAT	ENDANGERED
SAN MARTIN ISLAND WOOD RAT	ENDANGERED
KEY LARGO WOOD RAT	ENDANGERED
SAN JOAQUIN VALLEY WOOD RAT	VULNERABLE
SILVER RICE RAT	INDETERMINATE
KEY LARGO COTTON MOUSE	ENDANGERED
CHOCTAWATCHEE BEACH MOUSE	ENDANGERED
ALABAMA BEACH MOUSE	ENDANGERED
SOUTHEASTERN BEACH MOUSE	INDETERMINATE
ANASTASIA ISLAND BEACH MOUSE	ENDANGERED
PERDIDO KEY BEACH MOUSE	ENDANGERED
SOUTHERN MARSH HARVEST MOUSE	VULNERABLE
COLORADO RIVER COTTON RAT	ENDANGERED

Jeff Foott/Survival Anglia

THE HABITAT OF THE SALT MARSH HARVEST MOUSE IS THREATENED BY POLLUTION AND DEVELOPMENT.

● As nations begin to take pride in their wildlife heritages, there is a trend toward protecting wildlife even in the most inconspicuous forms.

Black rats have caused the decline of many other Galápagos species, such as tortoises, seabirds, and reptiles. However, they have had a less detrimental effect on the fauna of those islands, which had already been supporting populations of rice rats. This is because the ecological niche occupied by the rice rats has been taken over almost completely by the black rats. Rice rats remain the only Galápagos land-based mammals not imported by humans.

The Galápagos giant rat was another victim. This species is now known only through bones and teeth found in 1962 in a cave on Santa Cruz Island. It was considerably bigger than the South American giant water rat (the largest living hesperomid species), with a head-to-tail length of some 27.5 inches (70 cm). This species had evolved entirely in the absence of predatory mammals and would have offered no resistance to the introduced domestic cats and dogs—or to the *Rattus* species.

Many Caribbean species have also been wiped out in relatively modern times. Three species of West Indian giant rice rats once ranged across the Lesser Antilles. These rats were comparable in size to the Galápagos giant rat. They were officially declared extinct after the devastating volcanic eruption of Mount Pelée on Martinique in 1902. It is more likely that they had already been exterminated by coconut plantation owners, who saw them as a threat to their livelihood.

A large specimen of *Peromyscus*, the deer mouse genus, is known only by some 2,000-year-old bones found on San Miguel Island off the southern California coast. Some scientists have argued that this was the first North American mammal to become extinct as a result of human habit modification. The evidence seems to be circumstantial, based largely on the coinciding of Native American settlement with the age of the bone remains. It seems more likely that the mouse species survived until the 1860s, when overgrazing of sheep stripped the natural vegetation of the island.

These large specimens still attract attention long after their extinction. But the majority of New World rats and mice are small and nocturnal; those whose habitats overlap with humans' are usually discreet, and there are certainly many microhabitats that are removed from direct human contact. Zoologists can only speculate about the number of species yet to be classified. The corollary is that they must also speculate about how many species have already become extinct before they had even become known to scientists.

The silver rice rat is a Caribbean species that has been found only on the Keys of southern Florida. It was discovered as late as 1973 but is already scarce because its wetland habitat is under threat. The World Conservation Union classifies the silver rice rat as "indeterminate." Several related rice rat species of the genera *Oryzomys* and *Megalomys* died out on Caribbean Islands in the 19th century. They fell victim largely to small Indian mongooses, which were introduced to control plagues of both black and brown *Rattus* species, which were themselves wreaking havoc upon the sugarcane plantations. In all, the introduction of species—whether by accident

ALONGSIDE MAN

GOOD TIMES, BAD TIMES

New World rats and mice have sometimes suffered from bad press. Sudden population surges, as experienced by cotton rats in Honduras in 1974–1975, can lead to widespread losses of sugarcane, corn, millet, cotton, and rice. But the Honduras experience was exceptional, following heavy rainfall and a fierce hurricane that upset much of the normal food cycle.

Farmers view other species, such as rice rats and harvest mice, as nuisances or serious pests, but the damage they cause is nothing when compared with their introduced Old World counterparts. It is safer to claim, if any generalization can be made of a subfamily with nearly four hundred species, that New World rats and mice usually coexist peacefully with humans.

Deer mice are often used in science but the common house mouse and common rat, Old World species, have made even greater contributions to scientific research.

Cotton rat numbers rise and fall with the seasons. During peak population times, they can become serious agricultural pests.

or design—has spelled doom for countless indigenous island animals that had evolved in peaceful isolation for thousands of years. Another example involves not rats but goats, on the island of Santa Catalina off California. Brought to the island in the early 19th century by traders, they quickly established massive feral populations and, along with the local sheep and cattle, stripped the island of much of its vegetation. Among those native species that suffered greatly as a result were Slevin's deer mouse and the western harvest mouse.

MAINLAND SURVIVORS

Most mainland rice rats are generalists, and some have coped well with human development. They resemble deer mice in overall number (about fifty species) and in their ability to cope with a wide range of habitats—including marshland, forests, grassy areas, and scrub highlands.

The arrival and spread of human settlements have not seemed to damage the survival rate of most mainland rice rats. Overall, they seem capable of abandoning virgin woodlands for wheat fields in North America and tropical forests for sugarcane plantations in South America.

The up-and-down fortunes of genera such as the deer mice and rice rats mirror the survival of the hesperomid subfamily as a whole. Historically, those species locked into dwindling microhabitats have become isolated or have disappeared. But overall, these rats and mice have reacted successfully to habitat changes—naturally occurring and artificial—by adjusting their own habits. In their survival and development as a subfamily, they have shown that "the meek shall inherit the earth." ■

James H. Robinson/Oxford Scientific Films

INTO THE FUTURE

Keeping track of a subfamily as wide-ranging as the Hesperomyidae is bound to be a hit-or-miss business. Many threatened species live in isolated microhabitats, while others live near humans whose own standard of living is critically low. It is hardly surprising that governments largely ignore the needs of indigenous rodents whose only economic influence—as agricultural pests—has been negative.

The fate of New World rats and mice is not very newsworthy even in wealthier nations, where a raised standard of living seems to be a prerequisite for animal welfare concerns. It would take a skillful publicity campaign to raise the profile of, for example, Central American water rats to that of giant pandas, black rhinos, or mountain gorillas.

Yet there have been lone voices who have questioned the development of hesperomid habitats. The outcry about the fate of the salt marsh harvest

PREDICTION

PRESERVE THE MICROHABITATS

The patterns of the last century are likely to continue, with more island populations falling victim to development and to competition with Rattus. The fates of many species depend on the preservation of unique wetland and desert microhabitats.

mouse and the southeastern beach mouse has increased people's general awareness about these rats and mice—at least in the United States. It is too soon to say whether these species can be saved, but perhaps public concern might be compounded if more hesperomids were to come under threat.

Living in the shadow of more high-profile species might also benefit the subfamily. Any measures taken to improve conditions for the bobcat, the Florida panther, or the ocelot will indirectly help hesperomid populations in the relevant U.S. habitats. But there has also been increased concern about habitats in their own right. The decline in the numbers of North American ducks during the early 1990s is unparalleled since the 1930s. Duck populations have traditionally been seen as health indicators of the continent's ecosystems, and there have been calls for increased protection of wetlands. Again, any measures resulting from this concern will improve the position of the rats and mice that share such habitats. ■

STORM SURVIVORS

In September 1979, Hurricane David swept through the Caribbean region and the southeastern United States, leaving in its wake 1,100 people dead and thousands homeless. One of its most unsung victims, at least initially, was a deer mouse subspecies that had a natural home on a very narrow strip of the Gulf of Mexico between Alabama and northern Florida.

The devastation reduced numbers of this mouse to as few as twenty-nine in a survey taken soon after the hurricane. For a time it had the dubious honor of being named the rarest mammal in the United States. Since then numbers have increased, thanks to coastal wildlife protection and a reintroduction program. The latest count put the population at more than 100 and rising.

LAW ENFORCEMENT

One of President Ronald Reagan's last acts in office was the signing of the Endangered Species Act in 1989, which funded the monitoring of species not yet officially deemed threatened. The act was pushed through after concern about drought conditions in woodlands and wetlands; coincidentally, this wide range covered most hesperomid habitats. The act had enough bite to cancel or postpone some major projects: The Environmental Protection Agency rejected a proposal to build a recreation area at Lake Alma, Georgia, and levied heavy fines against three developers for illegally filling marshlands. However, the act expired in 1992 and has not yet been reaffirmed.

Illustration Deborah Pulley/Wildlife Art Agency

OLD WORLD RATS & MICE

RELATIONS

Rats and mice belong to the suborder Myomorpha, or mouselike rodents. Other members of this suborder include:

NEW WORLD RATS & MICE

AFRICAN CLIMBING MICE

HAMSTERS & GERBILS

VOLES & LEMMINGS

JERBOAS

BLIND MOLERATS

Ken King/Planet Earth Pictures

THE PATTER OF TINY FEET

FOR CENTURIES, RATS AND MICE ATE OUR FOOD, SPREAD DISEASE AND DEATH, AND GNAWED THEIR WAY INTO ALMOST EVERY ASPECT OF HUMAN LIFE. BUT HOW ARE THEY FARING IN THE MODERN WORLD?

R ats and mice produce mixed feelings in most people. They are a source of irrational fear; they spoil food intended for human consumption; they create fire hazards by gnawing at electrical wires. Yet when a cat catches a mouse, a person's first instinct is to rescue the quivering bundle and release it back into the wild.

Two species, the house mouse and the brown, or Norwegian, rat, have spread to every major continent. They live near human habitation and share food and shelter with us, and they have appeared in many legends and stories through the ages. But the house mouse and the brown rat are only 2 species of more than 400 different rats and mice from the Old World—Europe, Africa, Asia, and Australasia—that make up the subfamily Murinae; most of these live in tropical woods and forests and are seldom seen. As well as this subfamily, there are more than 90 other species of Old World rats and

mice and many more from the New World.

The tiniest member of the Murinae subfamily, the pygmy mouse, has a body as small as a human thumb and weighs just 0.2 oz (6 g). The largest, Cuming's slender-tailed cloud rat from the Philippines, has a body that measures 19.7 inches (50 centimeters) long and a tail to match.

RAMPANT RODENTS

Old World rats and mice are rodents. The order Rodentia, with about 1,700 species, contains almost half of all mammal species. Their hallmark is a pair of large, gnawing incisor teeth situated at the front of the mouth, which grow continuously throughout the animal's life.

ALL RODENTS HAVE A PAIR OF LARGE, GNAWING FRONT TEETH THAT NEVER STOP GROWING

Constant gnawing and biting keeps them sharp and keeps them from getting too long. Rodents use these teeth to gnaw into hard nuts and seeds, as well as to defend themselves and inflict injuries on attackers.

Other rodents include beavers, squirrels, voles, and chinchillas, as well as many that are called "rats" or "mice" because of their outward appearance but that belong to other groups of rodents.

Most rodents are compact and lightly built, with

Erwin & Peggy Bauer/Bruce Coleman Ltd.

Nasahiro Iijima/Ardea

The brown rat (right) *is one of the most successful of all mammals, abundant in Europe and the U.S.; the Japanese field mouse* (above) *is one of the rarest.*

IN THE NEW WORLD

Claude Steelman/Survival Anglia

There are about 366 species of rats and mice in the New World (the Americas). They belong to the subfamily Hesperomyinae (hes-per-o-MIE-in-ie) and have been separated from their Old World cousins for millions of years, evolving and adapting to their particular habitats and needs.

Despite this, their basic body plan is similar, though their cheek teeth, or molars, are different. The cusps of the New World species are rounder and arranged in two rows instead of three.

small, fragile bones which are easily destroyed, so their skeletons rarely form fossils. As a result, their fossil record is very scarce, leaving huge gaps, much guesswork, and plenty of unanswered questions. What remains there are indicate that the first rodents evolved approximately 50 million years ago, in the Eocene epoch. Finds in North America show them to be squirrel-like tree climbers.

THE ANCESTORS OF TODAY'S RATS AND MICE ORIGINATED IN SOUTHEAST ASIA ABOUT 20 MILLION YEARS AGO

The early ancestors of rats and mice probably began to appear about 20 million years ago. Studies of other fossils and of genetics suggest that they first lived in Southeast Asia and then spread throughout the whole continent.

Most of the evolutionary developments of rats and mice have happened in the last few million years. During this time, they have spread into almost every habitat except the highest mountains, the coldest poles, and the sea. They have taken to living in trees, burrowing under the ground, and swimming in marshes and lakes. In terms of sheer numbers, with more than 1,000 species, rats and mice are the most successful of all mammals.

There is no simple split between rats on one hand and mice on the other—the true picture is much more complicated. Most rats and mice look alike. They possess big, beady eyes; a whiskery nose; a small, furry body; limbs of roughly equal length; small toes tipped with claws; and a long, usually hairless tail. Their fur is usually gray or brown.

The behavior and habitats of rats and mice are also very similar. Their standard foods are seeds,

---

RATS AND MICE DO NOT FALL INTO TWO EASILY DEFINED CATEGORIES—MOST OF THEIR CHARACTERISTICS ARE SHARED

---

nuts, fruits, grasses, and other plant parts, supplemented with the occasional small insect. Most are nocturnal, or active at night. They are agile, nervy, and alert, and quick to dash for cover. They are usually quite small, and, if caught, they have few defenses other than their sharp incisor teeth. Their survival as a species depends chiefly on breeding rapidly and plentifully—something at which they are very accomplished. ■

ANCESTORS

ISCHYROMYS

The creature known as *Ischyromys* (iss-kee-RO-miss), which was among the first of all rodents, lived about 50 million years ago. It had a characteristically mouselike shape; flexible, manipulative forelimbs and strong hind paws; and the large upper incisors typical of all rodents. Its squirrel-like tail suggests that it may have been more at home in the trees than its modern-day descendants, and it probably competed successfully with the primates living at the same time.

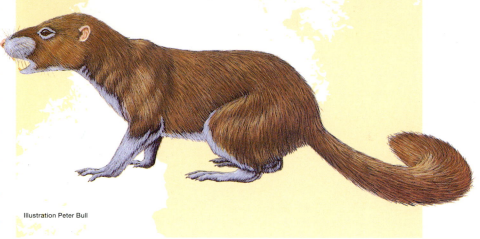

Illustration Peter Bull

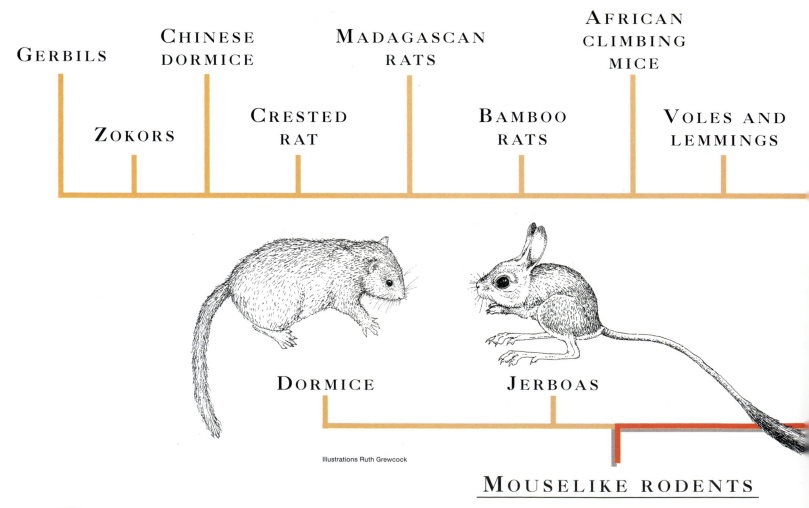

GERBILS

CHINESE DORMICE

MADAGASCAN RATS

AFRICAN CLIMBING MICE

ZOKORS

CRESTED RAT

BAMBOO RATS

VOLES AND LEMMINGS

DORMICE

JERBOAS

Illustrations Ruth Grewcock

MOUSELIKE RODENTS

HOUSE MOUSE AND BROWN RAT

Mus musculus (muss MUSK-yu-luss)

Rattus norvegicus (RAT-uss nor-VEJ-i-kuss)

The house mouse (below left) and the brown rat are among the most common of all the Old World rats and mice; they are widely regarded as pests.

Illustration Barry Croucher/Wildlife Art Agency

THE RATS' AND MICE'S FAMILY TREE

This tree shows how the Old World rats and mice (Murinae) are related to the other rats and mice. The rat and mouse family contains over 1,000 species and belongs to the suborder of mouselike rodents. Close relatives of the Murinae are the rats and mice of the New World and the ten other subfamilies of Old World rats and mice, some of which have evolved in isolation, like the Madagascan rats, and others, such as the blind mole-rats, which have taken to specialized ways of life. Most of these animals are very similar in terms of appearance; the major differences between the subfamilies are found in the details of teeth and jaw muscles.

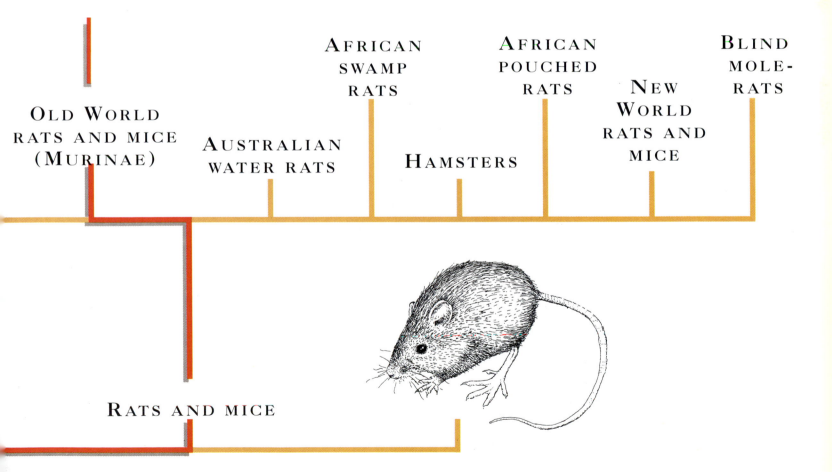

OLD WORLD RATS AND MICE (MURINAE)

AUSTRALIAN WATER RATS

AFRICAN SWAMP RATS

HAMSTERS

AFRICAN POUCHED RATS

NEW WORLD RATS AND MICE

BLIND MOLE-RATS

RATS AND MICE

JUMPING MICE AND BIRCH MICE

ANATOMY:
THE BROWN RAT

BROWN RAT

HOUSE MOUSE

THE RAT'S EARS

are large and prominent. Rats have a sharp sense of hearing, vital to a small animal hunted by larger predators.

The brown rat's body is about one foot long—a human foot, that is. Head-and-body length is 9–10.6 in (230–270 mm), and the tail is 7–8.7 in (180–220 mm). A house mouse is about one-third the size, or about 3.2–3.6 in (80–90 mm) long.

The muzzle of the brown rat is blunt and wedge-shaped, while that of the house mouse is pointed. Another difference: While a rat's ears sit neatly against its head, the ears of mice are more prominent and far larger in proportion to the head.

SENSITIVE SKIN

on the muzzle, and long whiskers that detect the slightest movement, allow the rat to feel its way in the darkness of night. The animal can assess the size of holes and cracks using its whiskers, and it can tell in advance whether they are wide enough to pass through.

THE FRONT, OR INCISOR, TEETH

are typical of any rodent. They are long and chisel-shaped, with strong, deep roots. The teeth grow continuously but are kept short and sharp by the animal's constant gnawing and biting.

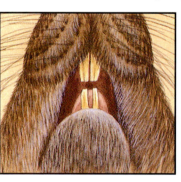

THE FRONT PAWS

are tipped with four claw-shaped nails. The toes can bend to cling when climbing and to hold and manipulate food. The feet are also used to dig holes, handle nesting material, and scratch enemies.

Illustrations Barry Croucher/Wildlife Art Agency

The rat's skeleton is made up of relatively thin and light bones, which give the creature a flexible body that can squeeze through surprisingly small gaps and holes. The rear legs are slightly longer and stronger than the front ones, able to propel the rat quickly away from danger.

SKELETON

curved, flexible spine

long tail

large hind feet

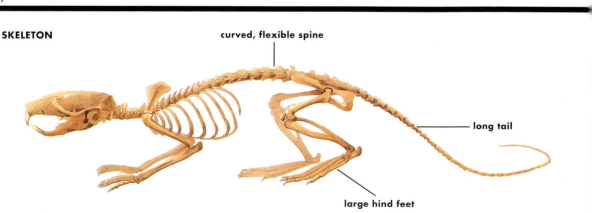

X-ray illustrations Elisabeth Smith

PAW PRINTS
of a mouse (right) and a rat (far right) show the differences between the forepaws, which have four toes, and the hind paws, which have five.

FACT FILE:

THE BROWN RAT

CLASSIFICATION

GENUS: *RATTUS*

SPECIES: *NORVEGICUS*

SIZE

HEAD–BODY LENGTH/MALE: 9–10.6 IN (230–270 MM)

WEIGHT/MALE: ON AVERAGE 7–14 OZ (200–400 G), ALTHOUGH 17.5 OZ (500 G) IS NOT UNLIKELY

ADULT MALES ARE ABOUT 40 PERCENT LARGER THAN FEMALES

COLORATION

FUR VARIES FROM GRAY-BROWN TO BLACK OR, IN SOME CASES, YELLOWISH

AT BIRTH RATS HAVE NO FUR—THEIR SKIN IS PINK AND WRINKLED

FEATURES

COARSE, SHAGGY FUR

TAIL IS HAIRLESS AND COVERED WITH SMALL SCALES

HIGHLY SENSITIVE NOSE, LONG WHISKERS AND PROMINENT EARS

BLACK, BEADY EYES THAT PROTRUDE FROM THE HEAD

THE TAIL
is relatively thick and not as long as its body (unlike that of the black rat). The tail's scaly skin is sensitive to touch, and the rat uses it to feel surfaces and textures and as a balancing aid.

THE RAT'S HIND PAWS
are longer and much stronger than its forepaws. Some species of rats are very capable swimmers and use their hind paws like paddles.

SKULLS FROM UNDERNEATH

incisors

molars

diastema

BROWN RAT   **HOUSE MOUSE**   **BROWN RAT**   **HOUSE MOUSE**

The skulls of both the rat and the mouse clearly display the gnawing, ever-growing incisors common to all rodents. The molars are used to grind and chew food. There is a considerable gap, or diastema, between the incisors and molars.

STRANGERS IN THE NIGHT

DESPITE THEIR NUMBERS AND THEIR PROXIMITY TO HUMANS, RATS AND MICE DO NOT LEND THEMSELVES TO CLOSE STUDY. SECRETIVE, NOCTURNAL CREATURES, THEY FLEE AT THE FIRST SIGN OF DANGER

The mice and rats of the Old World are essentially night creatures. Many are completely nocturnal, emerging from their burrows, nests, or resting places only after darkness has fallen.

On constant alert, their sharp senses are tuned in to suspicious sights, sounds, and smells. They have an intimate knowledge of their habitat and have escape runs or secondary burrows into which they dart in times of trouble.

They are not, on the whole, social creatures, though they may come together to feed on an abundant food source, and they may sleep together in communal nests during winter. At such times, they curb their natural aggressive tendencies toward each other and live in relative harmony.

INDIVIDUAL RATS AND MICE TEND TO BE AGGRESSIVE TO ONE ANOTHER. ONLY WHEN FOOD IS SCARCE IS THERE ANY SENSE OF COOPERATION

In general, each rat or mouse has its own home range and forages alone. Even where ranges overlap, as they do in many species, there is a "shift system"—each individual goes into the overlapping area at a different time and advertises its presence by marking and calling. Neighbors do not venture nearby while the overlap is occupied.

The daily routine varies according to the weather. If it is cold and wet, then the mouse or rat tends to stay in its shelter; but, if food is in short supply—during a drought, for instance—it may be driven to search for food more often than usual.

Despite the great number of different species, few rats or mice have been studied in any detail, and many that have been, such as the house mouse, brown rat, and black rat, have altered their patterns of behavior so much due to their long association with humans that they are no longer representative of rats and mice in their natural state.

The species that gives us the best idea of a typical day's behavior is the wood mouse, which is also called the long-tailed field mouse. It lives in the British Isles, southern Scandinavia, throughout mainland Europe and Central Asia, down to the coasts of North Africa, and into the Middle East.

STUDY BY FLASHLIGHT

The wood mouse has been closely studied largely because its eyes are not very sensitive to infrared light, and scientists can observe its habits by the light of a flaslight equipped with a simple red filter without disturbing the mouse.

The wood mouse's day begins about two hours before dusk, though if the weather is very cold and

Despite living alongside humans, the house mouse (right) is careful to keep its distance. The much rarer spiny mouse (above) feasts on a grasshopper.

Stephen Dalton/NHPA

Sean Morris/Oxford Scientific Films

On the up and up: A brown rat (below) *demonstrates its formidable climbing skill. The brown rat is among the most adaptable of all mammals.*

Daniel Heuclin/NHPA

damp, if there are unusual sounds that may indicate a predator, or even if the moon is bright, the mouse may delay emerging from its burrow. Rousing itself from sleep in its nest of dry leaves, moss, shredded grass, and other soft plant material, the wood mouse stretches, then licks clean its eyes, ears, paws, whiskers, and fur.

WHEN FORAGING, RATS AND MICE ARE
ALWAYS ON THE ALERT FOR PREDATORS
SUCH AS CATS, OWLS, AND WEASELS,
WHICH POSE REAL THREATS

In the summer, the peak feeding time is just before sunset. In winter, the activity tends to be split between a few hours after dusk and a few more before and during dawn.

The mouse sniffs and feels its way around, searching for food, constantly aware of the dangers presented by cats, owls, and weasels. If it finds a large supply of food, such as a tree bearing fruit, it may make several trips back to the burrow.

By the time most of the animal world is waking, the wood mouse has finished its day, and it is probably curled up, fast asleep in its burrow. In this way, millions of rats and mice go through their secretive lives under cover of darkness. ∎

HABITATS

Almost all the world's main land habitats have mouse and rat inhabitants. These ubiquitous rodents survive in alpine pasture, rocky uplands and moors, temperate and coniferous forests, shrubland and grassy savannas, arid scrub and semidesert, steamy tropical rain forests, marshes, and banksides. The distribution of the house mouse, the brown rat, and the black rat has been further increased by their links with humans; they travel by ship, road, railroad, and even airplane.

THE DRY SAHARA SUPPORTS VERY FEW RATS AND MICE, BUT IN THE GRASSLANDS OF AFRICA THERE MAY BE 10 OR 15 SPECIES IN ONE SMALL AREA

In Europe, there are only about eight species of mice, five of which—the wood mouse, the rock mouse, the pygmy field mouse, the yellow-necked mouse, and the striped field mouse—belong to the genus *Apodemus* (app-o-DEE-muss).

Each of these species has its own habitat preferences. The wood mouse is probably the most common and adaptable, ranging from dry sand dunes to parks and gardens, scrubland with bracken and brambles, woods, and farmland. It eats almost anything at any time of year.

In slightly more specialized habitats, however, the other species flourish at the expense of the wood

ZEFA

DISTRIBUTION

KEY

- **HOUSE MOUSE & BROWN RAT**
- **WOOD MOUSE**
- **STRIPED GRASS MICE**
- **RUFOUS-NOSED RAT**

Opportunists in the extreme, the house mouse and the brown rat have spread throughout the world with very few exceptions. They are absent from the extreme polar regions, which are too cold, and areas where competition from other small mammals is too fierce, such as central Africa.

The wood mouse is found in various types of woodland habitats throughout the British Isles and Europe, except for Scandinavia and Finland, and is found through the eastern Altai and Himalayan mountains.

Striped grass mice live in central and southern Africa, where they thrive in grasslands, prairies, dry wooded areas, and savannas.

The rufous-nosed rat is found in the forested regions and dense woodlands of western Africa, the Congo Basin, and bordering areas.

With a taste for almost any type of food, the wood mouse rarely has trouble finding enough to eat in its woodland habitat, even during the winter months. Here, a small piece of fungus makes a tasty snack.

mouse. The determining factors include types of food, food availability through the season, and types of shelter and nesting sites.

The rock mouse thrives in dry, rocky places in southeastern Europe, such as stony hillsides, dry scrubland, and even stone walls. The yellow-necked mouse is found across Europe and can live in many of the habitats occupied by the wood mouse, but it is a better climber and thrives also in conifer forests.

The striped field mouse, widespread in eastern Europe, prefers damp, lowland places, where it digs in the soil and spends most of its time underground. It eats worms, grubs, and small snails, specializing in animal food more than its relatives do.

East and south from Europe, the numbers of Old

● **Adaptations to habitat shape physical characteristics, from the strong claws of Peter's arboreal forest rat for gripping trees to the huge ears of hopping mice, which give off excess heat.**

● **Highest densities of Old World rats and mice species occur in countries with tropical forests. For example, the Philippines has 32 species; Uganda, 36; and Zaire, 44.**

● **The most successful of all mammals, Old World rats and mice are found in Europe, Asia, Africa, and Australia.**

World rat and mouse species rise rapidly in their main habitat—tropical woods and forests. Countries such as Uganda and Zaire have around thirty to forty species, as do India, the Malaysian region, Papua New Guinea, the Philippines, and Australia.

OUT OF SIGHT

Being small and fairly defenseless, rats and mice rely on their senses, agility, and camouflage to escape detection. As with many hunted animals, the color of their fur blends in with their surroundings.

Many scrub and semidesert species, such as the hopping mice of Australia, are light brown, fawn, or yellow to blend in with the light, sandy soil and pebbles. The hopping mice also show other

The stripes on the back of this Cape striped mouse (above) *are clearly visible; they act as camouflage in its grassland habitat.*

An African giant pouched rat (left) *decides whether cocoa pods are good enough to eat.*

adaptations to their semidesert habitat, including large hind legs for leaping across the open terrain and big ears—not only for acute hearing, but also to give off excess body heat in the hot conditions.

In contrast, the African swamp rats of the genus *Malacomys* (mal-a-CO-miss) are adapted for a watery life. Their hind feet have long, widely splayed toes for walking on soft ground, and their fur is thick and well coated with natural skin oils to repel water. Their coat is also dark brown to merge with the shady, muddy environment.

HOMEMAKERS

Most rats and mice build nests, the site and construction of which vary according to habitat. In grassland, nests are usually made in burrows and lined with shredded grass and other plant matter. The four-striped grass mouse of central and southern Africa digs a burrow up to over 3 feet (1 meter) long. This mouse has dark lines along its back, which camouflage it among the grass stems.

In woodlands, nests may be made in trees. The yellow-necked mouse often makes its nest in the crook of a branch or under a log. Peter's arboreal

FOCUS ON
THE MAYANJA FOREST

The lush, tropical habitat of Uganda's Mayanja Forest is not only home to some of the most varied and unique wildlife, but it is also a place where more than a dozen rat and mouse species thrive.

Here, competition is reduced by the way each species prefers a different minihabitat and has its own particular requirements. These minihabitats range from high tree branches, to bushes, to the ground, and spread from thick forest, to forest edge, to grassy clearing, to the bank of a pool or stream. Where two or more species occupy the same minihabitat, they coexist by eating different types of food.

The punctated grass mouse, for example, lives mainly on the ground alongside Peter's striped mouse; but the grass mouse is found in open, grassy areas, while the striped mouse prefers the forest interior. The long-footed rat ventures into swamps and streams to catch insects, frogs, and toads, while the climbing wood mouse feeds on seeds, fruits, and shoots in bushes and undergrowth.

TEMPERATURE AND RAINFALL

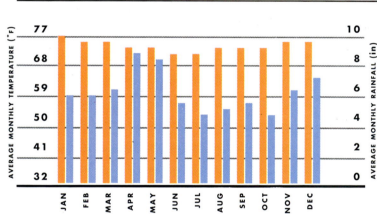

TEMPERATURE

RAINFALL

The temperature in African tropical forests ranges between 68°F (20°C) and 77°F (25°C) all through the year. Rain falls in all months, though it is concentrated in two periods, from March to May and October to December. Plentiful rainfall results in constant flowering and fruiting and rapid plant growth.

forest rat usually makes its nest in a tree hole and weaves it from creepers, twigs, leaves, and vines.

The pencil-tailed tree mouse lives in a variety of habitats, including bamboo thickets and plantations, where it nests in the hollow stems of the bamboo plant. It gnaws a hole about about 1 inch (25 millimeters) in diameter in the woody outer layer, cleans out the interior, collects various dry leaves for the nest, and sets up a home.

In contrast, the marmoset rat of Southeast Asia lives only among bamboo. It nests inside the stems, lines its nest with leaves, and feeds on all parts of the bamboo plant. Its wide-splayed toes are ideally suited for gripping the slippery stems. ∎

NEIGHBORS

Tropical conditions in Uganda's forests promote rich and varied flora and fauna. These creatures, from insects to exotic birds to grazers, share their homes with the numerous rats and mice there.

GIANT SNAIL

TREE PANGOLIN

The giant snail feeds on forest vegetation, scraping off bite-sized pieces of leaves with its rough tongue.

The scaly skin of the tree pangolin acts like a suit of armor, protecting it from its enemies in the trees.

Illustrations Peter Bull

ENEMIES

THE MAYANJA FOREST

Uganda is situated in central Africa between the Congo Basin and the Great Rift Valley. It is bordered by Kenya, Zaire, Tanzania, and Sudan.

To the west of Uganda's Lake Victoria lies the Mayanja Forest —a tropical region where rainfall and temperatures are high throughout the year.

EXTREMELY DANGEROUS

PYTHON
This extremely long snake grabs small mammals in its jaws and swallows them whole.

EXTREMELY DANGEROUS

GABOON VIPER
This extremely poisonous snake injects its venom into its victim using 2 in (5 cm) long fangs.

MODERATELY DANGEROUS

GOLIATH FROG
Up to 12 in (30 cm) long, this huge frog sits patiently waiting for its unsuspecting prey.

Ardea

LUNA MOTH

This huge moth wards off enemies with the eyespots on its wings, which look like two sets of staring eyes.

WATER CHEVROTAIN
This shy little creature rests by day and grazes at night. It is always found near water, hence its name.

GRAY PARROT

With a screeching call, the gray parrot flies swiftly and skillfully through the high canopy of the forest.

MILLIPEDE

The millipede has an unusual defense: When threatened, it oozes a foul-smelling liquid from its exoskeleton.

CROWNED EAGLE

An awe-inspiring predator of the forest canopy, the crowned eagle swoops down on monkeys in the branches.

FOOD AND FEEDING

Old World rats and mice are primarily herbivores—their diet consists chiefly of plant material. But, as with habitats, the key to the group's success is an adaptability to eating all kinds of food items, from leather to soap, eggs to carrion.

The much-studied wood mouse is a typical example. It could be called an omnivore—that is, it will feed on both plant and animal matter. It can also be termed an opportunist, because it will adapt to different foods as their availability and abundance change with the seasons.

MANY MICE AND RATS ARE OMNIVORES, OPPORTUNISTS THAT WILL EAT ALMOST ANYTHING THAT IS AVAILABLE

Given a choice, the wood mouse might select fresh, juicy seeds and fruits. It is particularly fond of cereals, such as wild oats and wheat, and berries, such as blackberries, as well as the ripe, sweet corn grown more widely in Europe.

As for animals, the wood mouse takes small earthworms, wood lice, insects such as beetles and moths, various grubs and larvae, and small spiders. It even tackles the armored millipedes and poison-fanged centipedes, and it will nibble away the shell of a snail to get to the flesh.

In spring and early summer, the wood mouse has a choice of a huge variety of new plant growth, including buds, shoots, and soft stems. It also catches caterpillars and grubs. As the year progresses, it

THE WOOD MOUSE

will nibble on insects as well as plant matter. It often eats in the branches of trees, relatively free from the unwanted attention of predators.

THE HARVEST MOUSE

(right) *eats a wide variety of nuts and seeds. It cracks open shells or seeds along their lines of weakness with its chisel-like incisor teeth.*

in SIGHT

SEWER LIFE

Though there is no such species as a "sewer rat," many rats do live in sewers. In Europe these are usually brown rats, and they live on almost anything, feeding on vegetable peelings, bits of bone and gristle, and other leftovers that get washed down the drain. They also eat the starchy substances found in paper and glue, and pieces of soap and wax. They are the supreme omnivore.

The sewers offer the rats good protection from the weather, shelter from predators, and a ready supply of food, but the rats hasten the collapse of sewers by tunneling into them.

Stephen Dalton/NHPA

turns more to fruits, nuts, and berries, such as hawthorn, acorns, and hazelnuts, and grass and cereal seeds. During winter, it relies mainly on nuts and seeds. In its varied and extensive menu, the wood mouse is typical of its group. Like others, it always approaches potential food with great caution, taking a small test nibble with its sharp front teeth and tasting the food with its tongue and mouth. If all is satisfactory, it nibbles some more, then chews with its broader back teeth before swallowing.

A HARD NUT TO CRACK

Soft foods may be swallowed almost at once, to save time while the mouse is exposed in the open. It cracks open hard-cased animals such as snails and beetles and licks out the soft flesh. Like many rats and mice, it can hold and manipulate food items using its front paws.

When a lot of hawthorn berries or acorns fall from the trees on a windy day, the wood mouse will pick these up in its front teeth and scurry back to its burrow. Here it stores the food in one or more "larder" chambers, ready for any future food shortages.

For the average rat or mouse, about half of its waking time is spent feeding—about four to six hours each night. The rest of its time is occupied with searching for food, cleaning and grooming, marking territory, maintaining the nest and burrow, and other everyday activities.

WATER SUPPLY

Rats and mice will drink water when available, but more or less depend on the moisture content of their food. They often get much of their liquid requirements from soft, fleshy berries and the blood and body fluids of caterpillars and grubs. ■

AMAZING FACTS

● About half of the species of Old World rats and mice are herbivorous.

● Mice and rats are great hoarders of food. A house mouse can easily amass a pile of food ten times bigger than itself.

● Cannibalism is not unknown. If they are lacking protein in their diet, brown rats instinctively eat their own kind.

THE COMMON RAT

(below) *will eat almost anything. This one has just caught a frog, a protein-rich catch for an animal that must eat one-third of its body weight each day.*

Illustrations John Morris/Wildlife Art Agency

LIFE CYCLE

There are two main reasons why rats and mice are so successful. They breed very quickly and they have developed various patterns of behavior to cope with the many dangers that threaten them.

Rats and mice are so small and defenseless that even the environment in which they live can be an enemy. Periods of cold or heat, lack of food, and drought may endanger their survival. The best way to cope with all these is to hide from them.

SAVING ENERGY

Some rats and mice, such as dormice, jumping mice, and birch mice, are true hibernators. Their body processes slow way down. Body temperature drops to just a few degrees above the temperature of their surroundings, as low as 41°F (5°C). Their heart rate slows from the usual 300 beats or more per minute to only a few beats per minute. Likewise, breathing and other body processes, such as digestion and urine formation, become slower.

The hibernation strategy saves energy during the cold season. The typical hibernating mouse lives through the winter on its stored reserves of body fat, safe in a well-insulated nest.

Frank Park/NHPA

DOWN UNDER

Lack of water affects rats and mice in desert conditions, such as the Australian hopping mice of the genus *Notomys*. Like some other desert animals, they stop up the entrances to their burrows during the fierce sun of the day to prevent the heat from coming in and the cool, moist air from getting out.

Hopping mice sleep in communal nest chambers. This maintains high humidity in the air, and so saves water loss.

On the other hand, Old World rats and mice are not true hibernators. This may be partly because the group is predominantly tropical, so there is no winter season for most of the species. But there are many other adaptations to harsh conditions, especially in the European and Australian species.

One of these is torpor. It is a "halfway house" to real hibernation, a deep sleep that is similar in some ways to true hibernation but not as profound. The

A WOOD MOUSE *spends most of the winter asleep in its underground burrow, waking every so often to feed on its store of acorns and seeds.*

wood mouse is one species of the Murinae that occasionally falls into torpid sleep during the winter. Its body temperature falls by 9 to 18°F (5 to 10°C), and its heartbeat and breathing slow down, too.

TAKING IT EASY

This torpid condition of deep sleep may last for several days. The wood mouse does not go into the same condition as a true hibernator, but it does save energy, and so food. And it can rouse itself quickly to go out and forage if there is a mild spell. It also benefits from staying out of the way of hungry predators. Other species in the Murinae subfamily

The wood mouse's burrow is made up of a sleeping chamber, a "larder," and a network of tunnels.

may also go into a torpor, but very few have been studied as extensively as the wood mouse.

In the winter or during cold snaps, Old World rats and mice tend to stay in their burrows for longer periods. They store some food as body fat, in the manner of real hibernators, and also hoard food items in burrow chambers or "larders." Depending on the size of this store, they can survive for days in the nest burrow, emerging only to sip water or to rid their bodies of waste.

MORE OF THE SAME

In nature there are many strategies for successful breeding. One approach is to breed as fast as possible, producing lots of offspring that mature quickly, and lots of batches of offspring through the year. Biologists call this the r strategy.

The other option is to have only one or a few offspring and spend much time and effort taking

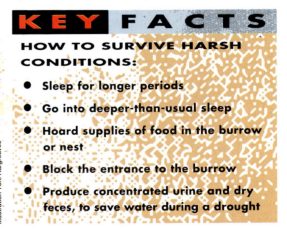

KEY FACTS

HOW TO SURVIVE HARSH CONDITIONS:

- Sleep for longer periods
- Go into deeper-than-usual sleep
- Hoard supplies of food in the burrow or nest
- Block the entrance to the burrow
- Produce concentrated urine and dry feces, to save water during a drought

1917

care of them, so that they get a slower but surer start in life. This is known as the K strategy.

Most mammals are somewhere in the middle of these two strategies, though humans as a species are very K-orientated, and rats and mice are very much at the r end of the spectrum. Their lifestyle revolves around producing large litters of young, and as many litters as possible. Youngsters rapidly reach adult size, become mature themselves, and begin to raise their own families.

One of the fastest breeders of the Murinae subfamily is the harvest mouse, which is also one of the smallest, with a body only 2.3 to 2.7 inches (60 to 70 millimeters) long.

Like many rats and mice from temperate regions, the harvest mouse begins breeding in the late spring. It has three or more litters through the summer, the last litter growing up in October or perhaps November. In tropical countries, where plants flower and fruit throughout the year, many species breed year-round.

UNDER CONSTRUCTION

The harvest mouse builds a spherical nest of tightly woven grass, leaves, and stems, with a single round entrance and a lining of shredded, chewed grass. About 4 inches (10 centimeters) in diameter, the nest is supported on the stems of grasses, reeds, or grains, or in brambles, about 12 to 24 inches (30 to 60 centimeters) above the ground.

The mouse lives in this type of nest year-round. But when it is not breeding, the nests are slightly larger and less compact and often closer to the ground, even at ground level or in a burrow.

After a brief courting ceremony, where the male pursues the female and makes chattering noises, the pair mates. She is pregnant for less than three weeks, and she may almost double her weight

IN THE NEST

newborn mice are hidden away in sturdy breeding nests. There is only a small entrance; the drawing (right) shows a cross section.

MATING MAY BE SILENT,

or it may be accompanied by the excited chattering noises of the female. She will probably have tried to elude the male several times before she lets him mount her.

AFTER FIFTEEN OR SIXTEEN DAYS,

the young mice are independent of their mother, and she is now pregnant with her next litter.

AMAZING FACTS

SUPER BREED

The multimammate rat (*Praomys natalensis* [pray-O-miss na-ta-LEN-siss]) from Africa is a really fast breeder. In fact, it gets its name from the numerous teats, or mammary glands, along its belly. It has up to ten pairs, compared to the normal four or five pairs that other mice and rats have.

A female multimammate rat breeds from the age of three months, has a gestation period of three weeks, may produce up to twenty babies in a litter, and may have litters at four-week intervals. No wonder these rats can quickly reach plague proportions!

GROWING UP
The life of a young harvest mouse

AFTER SIX DAYS,

the young have instinctively learned to lie still while being carried in their mother's teeth.

AT TWELVE DAYS OLD,

the young are able to see and move around in the nest. They may venture out to explore their surroundings.

Illustrations Ruth Grewcock

FROM BIRTH TO DEATH

HARVEST MOUSE	
GESTATION: 18–19 DAYS	**WEIGHT AT BIRTH:** 0.025 OZ (0.7 G)
LITTER SIZE: 1–8; USUALLY 4–6	**EYES OPEN:** 7–9 DAYS
NUMBER OF LITTERS PER YEAR: UP TO 8, USUALLY 2–4	**WEANING:** 15–16 DAYS
	SEXUAL MATURITY: 6–8 WEEKS
BODY LENGTH AT BIRTH: 0.5–0.75 OZ (15–20 MM)	**LONGEVITY:** 18 MONTHS; UP TO 5 YEARS IN CAPTIVITY

during this time. Smaller than the tip of a little finger, the babies are born naked with gray-brown skin. Their ears are tiny and their eyes closed. The mother feeds them with milk from her four teats. The babies grow quickly, their ears become more prominent, and their fur appears. By the time they are ten days old, they look more like mice and are able to wriggle around the nest and squeak for food.

RAPID DEVELOPERS
The mother cleans the nest and feeds her babies for about two weeks. Then the young are weaned on solid food such as seeds, grass stems and shoots, soft fruits, and tiny animals such as weevils. They leave home for good at three weeks old. If the mother has already mated again, she may chase them away so that she can concentrate on her next family.

HARVEST MICE THAT ARE BORN EARLY IN THE SEASON MAY BECOME MATURE ENOUGH TO RAISE THEIR OWN FAMILIES BY EARLY AUTUMN

In one season, one female harvest mouse can have up to eight litters of six babies each. This type of reproductive capacity is common to most species in the Old World group of rats and mice, so it is easy to see how numbers of these rodents can expand when conditions are good and predators are few.

The larger species of rats and mice tend to breed more slowly, but not by much. For the brown rat, the gestation period is twenty to twenty-three days, with an average of six to nine young born per litter, which are weaned after twenty-one days. In one survey, an average female produced twenty-four young each year, with a potential of more than fifty.

SHORT LIVED
Few rats and mice live long enough to grow old or develop diseases. They become prey to a huge variety of animals, from cats and owls to stoats and weasels, foxes and badgers, and even to larger species of their own group. Pest species are poisoned, trapped, and shot. In one survey on a farm, only one brown rat in twenty survived to reach its first birthday. ■

COMMON CONCERNS

WHILE BROWN RAT AND HOUSE MOUSE POPULATIONS OFTEN REACH PLAGUE PROPORTIONS, MANY TROPICAL SPECIES OF RATS AND MICE ARE SO RARE THAT THEY ARE KNOWN ONLY FROM THEIR REMAINS

Can there really be a problem with the survival of the Old World rats and mice? They are so common that in many places populations reach pest proportions. Their gnawing damages buildings, electrical wiring, and other installations. Their burrowing undermines banks, foundations, tunnels, and sewers. Their droppings contaminate food.

A house mouse produces about fifty droppings each day, and the brown rat about forty. Contaminated foods cannot be eaten because of the danger of disease. So why do these creatures deserve our sympathy and help?

THREAT OF EXTINCTION

The answer is that some particular species do not. But there are many other lesser-known species that are rare, even threatened with extinction. The single major threat is the loss of suitable habitat, especially tropical forests, which endangers so many of the world's animals and plants.

Other threats include predation from introduced species such as cats and foxes and competition from

> **VERY FEW RAT OR MOUSE SPECIES ARE PESTS, BUT, BECAUSE THEY ALL LOOK SO ALIKE, PEOPLE TEND TO GROUP THEM ALL TOGETHER**

introduced species of mice and rats. These problems are particularly associated with those rats and mice indigenous to Australasia.

One of the greatest dangers faced by rats and mice is that of human attitudes toward them. Though only a few species are responsible for disease and food spoilage, our antagonism to these species is such that it spreads to the whole group. The fact that many species look so similar makes it difficult for the layman to distinguish a house mouse or a brown rat from a rare local species. People tend to poison, trap, and shoot first, then identify later, if at all.

The main reason for the low public standing of rats and mice rests with their ability to spread disease. Some of the greatest pandemics (when diseases are prevalent over a large area), including bubonic plague, have been spread by the black rat. This is caused by a bacterium that is passed from person to person by the fleas that live on rats.

DEADLY DROPLETS

The bacteria can also be spread as droplets in the air. This particularly virulent form, pneumonic plague, was responsible for the vast outbreaks that killed about 100 million people in the 6th century

John Downer/Planet Earth Pictures

Rats make themselves at home in the insulating cavities of houses (right) *or by feasting on spilled grain* (above).

Liz & Tony Bomfield/Survival Anglia

The map below shows the former and current ranges of tropical rain forest in the Philippines, home to a number of rare species of rats and mice.

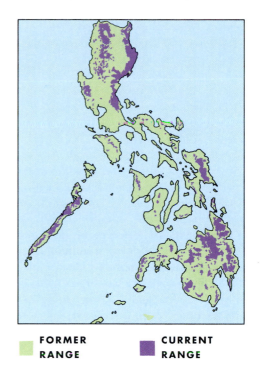

■ **FORMER RANGE** ■ **CURRENT RANGE**

Filipino rain forest remains only in isolated pockets in

- **Northern Luzon**
- **Palawan**
- **Eastern Cebu**
- **Southeast Mindanao**

A.D., and another 75 million during the Black Death of the 14th century. Small outbreaks of bubonic plague still occur. A vital part of its control is to continue to wipe out the local populations of infected rodents and their fleas.

LACK OF INFORMATION

The vast majority of Old World rats have little to do with the spread of disease and are far more likely to be under threat themselves. In fact, there is little detailed information on many of the rare species: They are hard to locate, and their favorite habitat of tropical forest makes observation difficult.

In the dry interior of the eastern and central states of Australia lives the long-haired rat, also called the plague rat. Many farmers detest it since they fear catching the plague, though there is absolutely no evidence that this particular species is responsible for spreading the disease.

Actually, the name comes from the fact that now and again, during the favorable conditions presented by a good rainy season, the rats breed very successfully, quickly reaching plague numbers. Almost as quickly, they outstrip their resources and run out of food. But the local predators multiply because of their own plentiful food supply of rats. Consequently, the population of long-haired rats falls back to normal.

A DIFFERENT STORY

The long-haired rat is, at present, holding its own, but many other Australian rat and mouse species have suffered different fates.

There were once ten species of Australian hopping mice; five of these are now thought to be extinct. The big-eared hopping mouse is known only from two specimens collected in the 1840s; it has never been captured or found since. The short-tailed hopping mouse was probably always rare, and only two living specimens were studied, in the 1930s. It seems to have vanished without a trace.

The long-tailed hopping mouse has had a much more spectacular demise. During the 1840s a naturalist working in Western Australia remarked that long-tailed hopping mice had a habit of raiding sacks of food in storerooms, and that they were especially fond of raisins. Its reputation as a pest spread, with devastating results—it has not been seen since 1901.

Because evolution is a continuing process, it is

Mary Evans Picture Library

The Great Plague of London in 1665 (above) was spread by the black rat. The Great Fire the following year brought an end to widespread plague in Britain.

ENDANGERED ENVIRONMENT

Nigel Cattlin/Holt Studios Intern

DEFORESTATION IN THE PHILIPPINES

Wherever tropical forests are being cleared for timber or farmland, rare species of rats and mice are under threat.

Nowhere is this more true than in the Philippines, where deforestation has drastically reduced the country's forest cover from about 42 million acres (17 million hectares) in 1930 to less than 17 million acres (7 million hectares) today. These tropical forests are prime habitats for rare rats and mice, not to mention thousands of other better-known species of animals, such as the rare monkey-eating eagle.

SPECIES IN DANGER

Deforestation has occurred mainly as a result of logging for valuable hardwood timbers, especially those of the dipterocarp species. As a result of commercial logging, the area of dipterocarp forests in the Philippines has fallen from 27 million acres (11 million hectares) 50 years ago to just 2.5 million acres (1 million hectares) today.

The problem in island groups such as the Philippines is particularly acute, because many of the species of rats, mice, and other creatures that live there occur

CONSERVATION MEASURES

Over the last 20 years, wildlife and environmental agencies have persuaded Philippine authorities that their forests are a tremendously valuable resource, not only for managed, sustainable timber production, but also as a home to rare and endangered species.

• Unauthorized logging is now banned in more than 40 of the Philippines' 73 provinces.

nowhere else, having evolved in isolation on the islands. It is estimated that 60 percent of the mammals on the Philippines are endemic, or original to that country. Thirty species of Old World rats and mice are found only in the Philippines, including the largest of all the Murinae, Cuming's slender-tailed cloud rat.

LACK OF INFORMATION

Whether these animals have a future is open to debate. As in most countries, in the Philippines rats and mice are regarded as pests or plague creatures, even when they are among the rarest and most endangered of species.

Panos pix

MODERN LOGGING HAS ALMOST DESTROYED THE PHILIPPINES' TROPICAL RAIN FOREST.

However, widespread illegal logging continues.

● The urgent need for such bans was highlighted in 1991 when around 6,000 people were killed by Typhoon Thelma. The mudslides that caused so many deaths were made worse because the hills had lost their tree cover owing to illegal logging.

RATS AND MICE IN DANGER

THE CHART BELOW SHOWS HOW THE INTERNATIONAL UNION FOR THE CONSERVATION OF NATURE (IUCN), OR THE WORLD CONSERVATION UNION, CLASSIFIES THE STATUS OF SOME OLD WORLD RAT AND MOUSE SPECIES:

GREATER STICK-NEST RAT	RARE
DUSKY HOPPING MOUSE	VULNERABLE

RARE MEANS THE ANIMAL HAS A SMALL WORLD POPULATION. VULNERABLE MEANS IT IS LIKELY TO BECOME ENDANGERED IF PRESENT CIRCUMSTANCES CONTINUE. ENDANGERED MEANS THE ANIMAL IS IN DANGER OF EXTINCTION.

Tony & Liz Bomfield/Survival Anglia

only natural that some species should be very common while others are in decline. In Australia in the late 18th century, however, the European settlers triggered a great acceleration in this process. The extinctions of the hopping mice, as well as seven other species of rodents, were caused by a number of interacting factors. These include the changes in plant cover caused by introduced rabbits and livestock; new predators in the shape of

---

AUSTRALIA'S RARE MOUSE AND RAT POPULATIONS FACE THE THREAT OF INTRODUCED ANIMALS AND A CHANGE IN PLANT COVER

---

introduced cats, foxes, and other species; and new competitors in the shape of introduced rats and mice, including the house mouse and brown rat.

This pattern of species loss may be occurring in many places across the Old World as rare, secretive, little-studied rats and mice succumb to the loss of their habitat, new predators, and more adaptable competitors. Unfortunately, the resources to conduct surveys, trap and identify species, and keep detailed records may not be forthcoming for such lowly and despised animals.

MISTAKEN ASSUMPTIONS

It is not all bad news, however. The harvest mouse is Britain's smallest rodent, easily identified by its grasping tail, which it uses as a fifth limb to clamber among the stems of vegetation. It has long been assumed that the numbers of harvest mice have been decreasing, especially since the introduction of combine harvesters in the 1950s.

However, a survey conducted in the 1970s by

ENDANGERED · ENVIRONMENT

ALONGSIDE MAN

A MOUSE IN THE HOUSE

Several species of Old World rats and mice live alongside humans, and they benefit in two ways. One is food. Being omnivorous opportunists, they are well placed to eat our leftovers and scraps, and also to invade supplies of grain or rice.

The other benefit is shelter and warmth. The black rat, for example, a common pest throughout the warmer parts of Asia, rarely lives in the open in temperate regions such as Great Britain, but it is more than able to survive in sheltered places such as port buildings and warehouses.

These select species have done well by their proximity to humans. After humans, the house mouse is the most widely distributed animal in the world, and it has even made it to Antarctica, where it lives in or near scientific settlements.

Jane Burton/Bruce Coleman Ltd.

The "throwaway," consumer society presents rats and mice with a constant supply of food.

the Mammal Society showed that harvest mice were not so rare after all. Their distribution was perhaps more restricted than in former times, but there were many thriving populations in grassy banks and hedgerows, vacant lots, bramble patches, and reed beds, as well as in fields of grain.

ADAPT AND SURVIVE

The harvest mouse's adaptability has enabled it to survive in reasonably healthy numbers, and the saddening image of the very last harvest mouse disappearing into the blades of a combine harvester is still a long way off.

Rats and mice have brought starvation and

Despite their reputations, rats make very good pets. These pedigree rats (below) are specially bred for human handling.

Hans Reinhard/Bruce Coleman Ltd.

plague, but they have also lent a helping paw. Like most animals that live close to man, they have been domesticated. Some people keep them as pets for their amusement, but they are also bred for more important—and controversial—reasons.

As laboratory "guinea pigs," they have had thousands of potential drugs and other medicines tested on them, as well as cosmetics, toiletries, and hundreds of other substances considered useful to man. Breeding studies on laboratory mice have also helped to unravel the mystery of gene inheritance.

One of the strangest stories is that of the Harvard mouse, or Onco mouse, which was genetically engineered to develop cancer, making it a useful subject for testing anticancer drugs. It was the subject of the first patent battle over who owns the rights to such genetically altered life forms.

> THE HARVARD MOUSE, BRED SPECIFICALLY TO DEVELOP CANCER, WAS THE SUBJECT OF THE FIRST PATENT BATTLE OVER ALTERED GENES

Despite their reputations, many people are very fond of rats and mice. Some may shudder at the thought of keeping one as a pet, yet those who do keep them are quick to point out the pleasures. Pet rats and mice have been bred for centuries, and, like any domesticated animal, their aggressive instincts have disappeared. Handled regularly, a pet rat or mouse becomes tame, docile, and easy to hold. Rats produce hardly any odor and, unless sick or old, keep themselves very clean. Because they have such a varied diet, they are also very easy to feed. ∎

INTO THE FUTURE

At present, there are no significant conservation or breeding programs aimed solely at saving species of Old World rats and mice. However, numerous species will benefit from any measures introduced to save their habitats, especially the tropical forests.

HABITAT LOSS

Loss of habitat is the biggest single threat facing wildlife today. Captive-breeding programs, along with bans on collecting and hunting, can contribute to a species' survival, but these measures cannot succeed unless there are natural wild places for the

PREDICTION

The future for Old World rats and mice will probably be much the same as the past. Though some little-known species may become extinct, especially in the tropics, the majority will continue their nocturnal, seed-eating lives, helped by the general conservation effort to preserve wilderness areas and to reverse habitat loss. The familiar few will continue to eat our food, gnaw our possessions, and spread disease.

animals to live. The focus is on preserving natural habitats intact, with their interlinked populations of plants and animals.

A particular problem affecting many rare rats and mice is competition from their own kind, especially from the infamous brown rat. Large, strong, and aggressive, the brown rat spreads to new areas and competes against the local rat species; it almost certainly take its place.

GREATER NUMBERS

One factor in the success of the brown rat is the similarity of the ecological niches occupied by many rat species. Brown rats occupy a large niche, owing to their wide range of foods and their tolerance to various climatic conditions. This enables them to survive and breed in greater numbers than a native species with more restricted requirements.

Another factor is that the brown rat has greater success at defending itself against introduced predators such as cats. So the elimination of introduced brown rats, along with the removal of introduced predators such as cats, is important for encouraging the survival of native rat species. ∎

AGENTS OF DISEASE

In recent years there has been an alarming increase in the numbers of cases of Weil's disease, particularly in developed countries such as the United Kingdom. This is a flulike disease carried in the urine of brown rats. Also called leptospirosis, it is caused by a spiral-shaped bacterium, Leptospira (lep-to-SPEER-ah). Weil's disease may be caught when swimming or working in water that has been frequented by infected rats, especially if the recipient has cut or broken skin. People whose work involves contact with water in rivers and lakes, or with sewage, are particularly at risk. Protective clothing offers the best means of avoiding the disease.

Other diseases on the increase, carried chiefly by the brown rat, include salmonella food poisoning and toxoplasmosis, a form of blood poisoning.

A LINK IN THE FOOD CHAIN

One of the reasons for conserving rat and mouse populations concerns their place in the food web. Mice in particular are a common item in the diet of many predators, some of which are themselves extremely rare.

A study of British owls in the 1980s showed that yellow-necked mice and wood mice formed about 12 percent by weight of the diet of the tawny owl, 14 percent of the long-eared owl's diet, and 10 percent of the barn owl's. Encouraging the abundance of mice and other small rodents can help conserve larger, high-profile hunters such as owls.

Illustration Kim Thompson

RHINOCEROSES

THE LIVING TANK

ITS LARGE SIZE, COUPLED WITH A SURPRISING TURN OF SPEED, THICK SKIN, AND A POTENTIALLY LETHAL WEAPON ON ITS NOSE, GIVE THE RHINOCEROS AN AIR OF INVULNERABILITY

With its massive, heavily muscled body, short neck, and magnificent horns, the rhinoceros looks almost prehistoric—and, in fact, it hasn't changed much over the last few million years.

The word *rhinoceros* means "nose horn," which is appropriate since rhinos are the only animals with horns on their noses—all other horned animals have their horns on the top of the head. There are five species living today: the black and white rhinos of Africa

and the Sumatran rhino, which all have two horns, with the front horn usually the larger; and the Indian and the Javan rhinos, which each have one horn.

Despite their name, rhino horns are not made of horn, nor do they have a bone down the middle, as cows' horns do. In fact, rhino horn consists solely of thousands of strands of tightly packed, incredibly strong, modified hair known as keratin. Size varies from species to species; the front horn of the southern white rhino can grow up to 6.5 ft (2 m) long.

CLASSIFICATION

Rhinoceroses belong to the order Perissodactyla and to the rhinoceros family or Rhinocerotidae. There are two subfamilies, the one-horned and the two-horned rhinoceroses.

ORDER
Perissodactyla
(odd-toed hoofed mammals)

FAMILY
Rhinocerotidae
(rhinoceroses)

SUBFAMILY
Rhinocerinae
(one-horned rhinos)

GENUS
Rhinoceros

INDIAN RHINO SPECIES
unicornis

JAVAN RHINO SPECIES
sondaicus

SUBFAMILY
Dicerorhinae
(two-horned rhinos)

BLACK RHINO GENUS
Diceros

SPECIES
bicornis

WHITE RHINO GENUS
Ceratotherium

SPECIES
simum

SUMATRAN RHINO GENUS
Dicerorhinus

SPECIES
sumatrensis

WHAT ARE UNGULATES?

Ungulate means an animal with hooves. Hooves—tough, horny outgrowths from the skin—result in longer legs, enabling the animal to run faster to escape from predators. Hooves also serve to protect the animal's flesh from hard or stony ground.

Ungulates are divided into two orders according to the number of toes that touch the ground: The Artiodactyla (ar-tee-o-DAK-till-a) have an even number of toes and include pigs, camels, deer, and cattle. The Perissodactyla (per-iss-o-DAK-till-a) have an odd number of toes and include rhinos, horses, zebras, and tapirs.

The black rhino's horns are honed to a polished point from being rubbed on trees and bushes. Its skin color is more gray than black, though its appearance depends more on the color of the local mud than on the pigment in the skin itself—visiting a wallow and covering itself with mud every day is an important part of a rhino's behavior.

The white rhino is the second largest living land animal after the elephant. Again, the name is not an accurate description of its color; it is a somewhat lighter gray than the black rhino, but it too is colored by the mud of its last wallow. It probably got

Masahiro Iijima/Ardea

Jean-Paul Ferrero/Ardea

The oldest rhino in evolutionary terms, the Sumatran rhino (above) has a hairy coat and ears, while the other species—including the Indian rhino (right)—are hairless.

its name from the Afrikaans word *weit*, which means "wide" and describes the shape of its mouth.

The Sumatran rhino's skin is slate gray and covered with short grayish black hairs. In captivity, the hairs grow longer—1 in (2.5 cm) or more—because they do not get worn down by rubbing against the dense vegetation.

ARMOR PLATING

The great Indian one-horned rhinoceros is the one that looks most like it is made up of plates of armor riveted together. The skin surface is, in fact, made up of studs of hard gray skin, but on a healthy rhino it is supple, not stiff. Though not as heavy as the

Illustration Alan Male/Linden Artists

ANCESTORS

INDRICOTHERIUM (in-drik-o-THEER-ee-um)
Most impressive of all the extinct rhinos was *Indricotherium grangeri*, the largest mammal ever to walk the earth. This huge, hornless rhino measured up to 30 feet (9 m) in length and weighed about 24.5 tons (22 tonnes) or, to put it another way, as much as four big bull African elephants put together! Unlike an elephant, however, it was not particularly intelligent: Its braincase was only a fraction of the size of that of a present-day rhino. *Indricotherium* stomped around the plains of what is now Mongolia until it died out about ten million years ago.

ELASMOTHERIUM (el-az-mo-THEER-ee-um)
The prize for the biggest horn must go to *Elasmotherium*. Its horn could grow as long as a man is tall and, at the base, almost as wide around. Such a large horn had probably resulted from sexual selection—females were attracted to the male with the biggest horn. Two males fighting head to head would have been a spectacular sight. It lived in Eurasia during the ice ages, and its size was an adaptation to cope with the cold. (A large animal has less surface area relative to its volume than a small one; most of an animal's heat is lost through the skin, so a large animal will lose less energy per pound of body weight than a small one.)

INDRICOTHERIUM

COELODONTA (seel-o-DONT-a)
In 1771 a huge carcass was found on the banks of a river in Siberia, half buried in frozen sand and gravel. It turned out to be the remains of a woolly rhino that had died in the last ice age. Patches of wool and bristly hair were visible on its hide, but both horns had gone. It was large and had a thick, shaggy coat—both adaptations to the bitter cold.

ELASMOTHERIUM   **COELODONTA**

white rhino, the Indian rhino may be taller; it can stand up to 6.5 ft (2 m) at the shoulder.

The Javan rhinoceros is midway in size between the Indian and Sumatran species. Its upper lip is long and its horn is small: less than 10 inches (25 cm) in the male and just a small knob in the female. Its gray skin is folded but lacks the knobbly appearance of the Indian rhino.

The rhino's ancestors include all sorts of strange creatures, not all of which had horns. The odd-toed ungulates split into two lines about fifty-four million years ago, at the beginning of the Eocene age. The horse family dates back to that time, but the line leading to rhinos and tapirs did not split until about

forty million years ago. The peak period for rhino ancestors took place between thirty-eight and twenty-six million years ago, in the Oligocene. This produced the line that led to the rhinos of today, as well as to other branches that died out when they could not adapt to further climatic changes. Twenty-five million years ago, the North American rhino failed to survive the spread of grasslands but, in Europe and Asia, many hoofed mammals moved south to Africa.

OVER THE PAST FORTY MILLION YEARS, THE RHINO FAMILY HAS SEEN A RICH AND DIVERSE ARRAY OF SPECIES

During the Pleistocene, when a succession of ice ages froze the Northern Hemisphere, rhinos were still found in Europe. They did not, however, survive the last ice age. Whether it was human hunting pressure that tipped the balance against them, as many scientists consider it did to the woolly mammoth, is open to question. ∎

WHITE RHINO
Ceratotherium simum (ser-at-o-THEER-ee-um SEE-mum)

The white or square-lipped rhinoceros can weigh as much as 8,000 lb (3,600 kg). It stands up to 6 ft (1.8 m) high at the shoulder and measures up to 14 ft (4.3 m) from head to tail.

SUBSPECIES:
NORTHERN
SOUTHERN

BLACK RHINO
Diceros bicornis
(die-SER-oss bie-COR-niss)

Also known as the hook-lipped rhinoceros, the black rhino can weigh up to 3,500 lb (1,600 kg) and measure 12.5 ft (3.8 m) in length. It stands about 6 ft (1.8 m) tall.

SUBSPECIES:

BUSHVELD	DESERT (OR CAPE)
CENTRAL AFRICAN	WESTERN

SUMATRAN RHINO
Dicerorhinus sumatrensis
(die-ser-o-REE-nuss soom-ah-TREN-siss)

The most agile of the rhinos, the Sumatran is also known as the Asian two-horned or hairy rhino. Adults measure 8–9 ft (2.4–2.7 m) in length and under 5 ft (1.5 m) in height.

SUBSPECIES:
NONE

Illustrations by Alan Male/Linden Artists

THE RHINOS' FAMILY TREE

Rhinos are in the same zoological order, the Perissodactyla, as horses and tapirs, but they are more closely related to the latter. The five species alive today fall into two subfamilies, classified according to the number of their horns. Those with one horn form the Rhinocerinae (rie-no-ser-EEN-ie), while those with two horns form the Dicerorhinae (die-ser-ro-REEN-ie).

JAVAN RHINO
Rhinoceros sondaicus (son-DAY-ick-uss)

Also known as the lesser one-horned Asian rhino, the Javan rhino attains a length of 11.5 ft (3.5 m) and a shoulder height of 5.75 ft (1.8 m). An adult male weighs 3,500 lb (1,600 kg) on average.

SUBSPECIES: NONE

INDIAN RHINO
Rhinoceros unicornis (yoo-nee-CORE-niss)

The Indian, or great one-horned, rhino is larger than the Javan, its somewhat primitive one-horned cousin. A massive animal, the Indian rhino weighs up to 4,400 lb (2,000 kg), reaching 14 ft (4.3 m) in length and standing 6.5 ft (2 m) high at the shoulder.

SUBSPECIES: NONE

HORSE

TAPIR

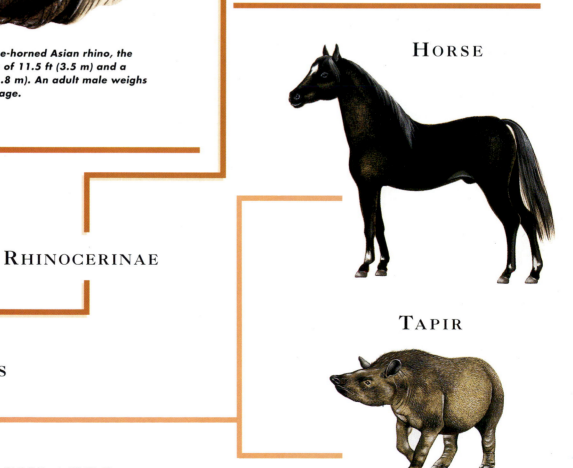

DICERORHINAE   RHINOCERINAE

RHINOS

ODD-TOED UNGULATES

1931

ANATOMY: THE RHINO

INDIAN RHINO **SUMATRAN RHINO**

The smallest rhino, the Sumatran, weighs in at a mere 2,200 lb (1,000 kg), while the heaviest is the white rhino (below), with an adult male tipping the scales at an average of 6,600 lb (3,000 kg)—the equivalent of over forty men!

THE HUMP

Long, bony spines stick up from the backbone on the back of the white rhino's neck. The massive muscles that lift the head are attached here, creating a hump.

INDIAN RHINO

THE EARS

can be moved independently, so when the rhino is in a vulnerable position—head down drinking, for example—it is common to see one ear pointing forward and one pointing backward.

The Indian rhino (above) has only one blunt horn, while the Sumatran rhino (below) has two; these are shorter and rounder than those of the white rhino (right).

SUMATRAN RHINO

THE HORNS

are anchored onto the head over a large bump on the front of the skull.

Illustrations Mathew Hillier/Wildlife Art Agency

X

R
A
Y

head carried low   long rib cage

WHITE RHINO SKELETON

front feet slightly larger than hind feet   short legs

The rhinoceros has an extremely robust and strong skeleton, which has evolved to take the enormous weight of its muscles and organs. Its long head is counter-balanced by the rest of its body. The white rhino has a longer head and shorter neck than the black rhino.

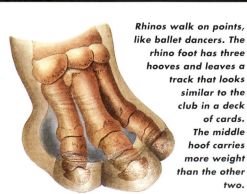

Rhinos walk on points, like ballet dancers. The rhino foot has three hooves and leaves a track that looks similar to the club in a deck of cards. The middle hoof carries more weight than the other two.

X-ray illustrations Elisabeth Smith

INDIAN RHINO

JAVAN RHINO

Both Indian and Javan rhinos have bumpy, hairless skin. The hide of the Javan rhino (left) looks scaly and has a mosaic pattern all over, while that of the Indian rhino (far left) is unevenly patterned. Its shoulder and upper leg areas are covered with wartlike bumps, while the rest is comparatively smooth.

FACT FILE

THE WHITE RHINO

CLASSIFICATION

GENUS: *CERATOTHERIUM*

SPECIES: *SIMUM*

SIZE

HEAD–BODY LENGTH/MALE: 12–14 FT (3.7–4.3 M)

TAIL LENGTH/MALE: 25 IN (65 CM)

HEIGHT/MALE: 5–6 FT (1.5–1.8 M)

WEIGHT/MALE: 5,000–8,000 LB (2,300–3,600 KG)

FRONT HORN LENGTH/MALE: ABOUT 28 IN (71 CM)

REAR HORN LENGTH/MALE: 9 IN (23 CM)

FEMALES ARE SMALLER AND LIGHTER THAN MALES

COLORATION

GRAY, TEXTURED SKIN, BUT USUALLY COVERED WITH MUD OR DUST

BLACK HAIR (EYELASHES, EAR FRINGES, AND TAIL)

FEATURES

LONG HEAD

POINTED EARS

BROAD, SQUARED-OFF MUZZLE

LARGE HUMP ON BACK OF NECK

THE TAIL

serves as a fly whisk and is equipped with a row of thick, black, wiry hairs that grow in a line along the underside and the top of the tip. Sometimes rhinos lose part or all of their tails if they are attacked by predators such as hyenas.

THE LEGS

are built like pillars to support its bulk. The long bones tend to rest in a straight line, enabling the rhino to stand without exerting too much energy.

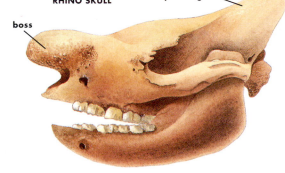

RHINO SKULL · occipital region · boss

Perhaps the most interesting feature of a rhino skull is the big bony mound, or boss, on which the horn grows. The occipital region at the back of the skull is long and deep, providing a firm attachment for the huge muscles, which are necessary to hold up the heavy head.

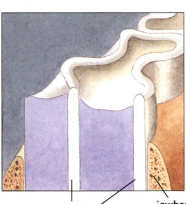

enamel folds · jawbone

A rhino's cheek teeth are designed for grinding up vegetation. Its molars and premolars in both upper and lower jaws have folds in the enamel surface. As they get worn down they form ridges (left), which shred food under the great pressure exerted by the jaws.

LIFE IN THE SLOW LANE

DESPITE THE OCCASIONAL SHOW OF AGGRESSION, RHINOS LIVE LIFE AT A LEISURELY PACE. MOST OF THEIR DAY IS TAKEN UP WITH EATING, SLEEPING, AND—THEIR FAVORITE OCCUPATION—WALLOWING IN MUD

The fearsome appearance of the rhino masks a gentle, largely passive creature. In fact, depending on the species, it spends most of its time grazing the African savanna or browsing through the forests and swamps of Africa, India, and Southeast Asia, feeding on an exclusively vegetarian diet. Though the sheer size and strength of the rhino can hardly fail to impress, the fact is that most rhinos (with the exception of the sometimes aggressive black rhino) would rather run from trouble than confront it.

Even the black rhino's occasional displays of aggression are largely due to its poor eyesight. Because it is too nearsighted to see if something is a

> **THE BLACK RHINO'S REPUTATION FOR AGGRESSIVE BEHAVIOR IS LARGELY DUE TO ITS POOR EYESIGHT**

threat or not, it tends to charge at everything in order to be on the safe side. Black rhinos have even been observed charging at trees in a vain attempt to scare them away.

Rhinos are ungulates, most species of which are preyed on by large carnivores. Many ungulates have evolved long legs, enabling them to escape at high speed from such predators. Rhinos, however, have taken a slightly different evolutionary path. Their great bulk, supported by short, stout legs and thick skin, evolved as alternative means of defense. So effective are the rhino's defenses that only man is a significant threat to a fully grown adult—though this threat alone may be one too many and could soon result in the extinction of every last rhino.

Rhinos are amazingly agile and run surprisingly quickly for their size: up to 30 miles (50 km) per hour. This is about the same speed as a horse, though rhinos cannot keep this pace up for long.

The Asian species are also excellent swimmers, able to cross the widest of rivers.

Despite these occasional physical exertions, rhinos are essentially easygoing, calm creatures. Like most mammals without hair, rhinos prefer to wallow away their days in pools of water and mud to escape the effects of the sun.

MUD BATHS

In India, where rhinos frequent swampy habitats, large groups or "crashes" of rhinos may remain submerged in the mud for several hours, staying there from noon until sunset. This normally cantankerous species displays an almost childlike pleasure in such activity.

When they finally emerge, they are covered in a protective mud coat that acts as a barrier against

ZEFA

Taking things easy: With the exception of humans, the rhino has no natural enemies in the wild and can spend most of its day sleeping (right) or eating (above).

Jonathan Scott/Planet Earth Pictures

HOW TO SURVIVE AN ANGRY RHINO

R. I. M. Campbell/Bruce Coleman Ltd.

What should you do if you are faced with an angry rhino? The temptation would be to run, but this might make matters worse. If the wind is blowing from the rhino's direction toward you, it might be best to freeze and wait motionless for the rhino to move off, as it will only be able to tell where you are by seeing or hearing you move. But if the rhino is suspicious and not sure of your exact whereabouts, it might or might not charge in your direction. Some claim it is better to face the beast rather than run, and be ready to dive to one side if it does happen to be on a collision course.

the bites of parasites and insects and keeps the rhino from getting sunburned. While the rhinos wallow, small terrapins and birds, such as cattle egrets and oxpeckers, feed on the swarms of insects found on the rhino's back. Soon after they have finished wallowing, rhinos may rub themselves against trees and rocks, another ploy to rid the skin of parasites.

LEISURELY LIFESTYLE

The calm, laid-back lifestyle of the rhino tends to be lived alone or in small temporary groups of up to about seven animals. In contrast, the relationship between the mother and her (usually single) young is among the strongest in the animal world.

Rhino calves stay with their mothers for years, learning all the skills necessary for their future survival. Rhino mothers are fiercely protective of their offspring: Tigers, among the most fearsome of predators, rarely get the chance to kill and eat an Indian rhino calf. Any tiger that attempts to do so risks the mother's lethal wrath in the form of her great bulk and huge horn. ∎

HABITATS

Gerald Cubitt/Bruce Coleman Ltd.

A solitary Sumatran rhino wades through a muddy swamp. Plenty of water and lush vegetation make this an ideal habitat for Asian rhinos.

W here an animal chooses to live is determined by its needs. Rhinos must have access to enough vegetation to maintain their bulk and, since all species except the black rhino need to drink every day, they must also have access to water.

SECRET NATURE

Consequently, prime rhino habitat must have good rainfall or a river or spring nearby that flows year-round. If the soil is low in salts there should also be a salt lick, a natural exposure of mineral-rich

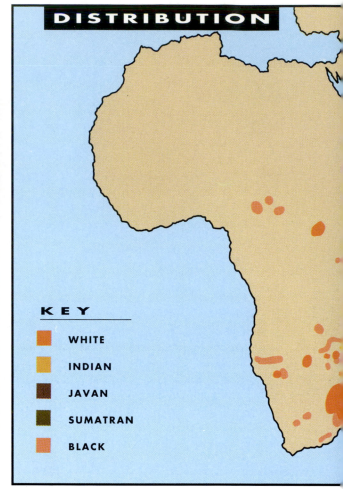

DISTRIBUTION

KEY

- ■ WHITE
- ■ INDIAN
- ■ JAVAN
- ■ SUMATRAN
- ■ BLACK

earth or rock, with which to supplement their diet.

The ancestors of the modern-day rhinoceros were forest-dwellers, and three of today's rhinos are found mainly in rain forests and woodlands. Scientists have recently suggested that the rhino's poor eyesight remained undeveloped because it was not of much use in a forest habitat where it is

> WHITE RHINOS SEEM CONTENT TO SHARE THEIR HABITAT WITH OTHER GRAZERS, EVEN THOUGH THEY ARE DIRECT COMPETITORS

difficult to see far in any direction. Two species, however, the white and the Indian, have evolved as grazers and so are found in open grassland, plains, or savanna habitats, providing there are clumps of trees or bushy areas to provide them with shade and cover.

The white rhino, as befits its reputation for gentleness, shows a great deal of tolerance toward the animals that share its habitat, even fellow grazers such as wildebeest, impala, and zebra, with which it competes for food. This is understandable

A black rhino browsing in the African grass-land. Black rhinos are able to adapt to a wider range of habitats than white rhinos.

Hans Reinhard/Bruce Coleman Ltd.

All the world's populations of rhinos have been decimated this century and almost all are isolated. Only Africa's white and black rhinos occupy a mutual habitat—in southern Africa. A population of about thirty northern white rhinos survives in Zaire, while Kenya, Namibia, Zimbabwe, and South Africa each have populations of a few hundred of the black species.

Of the Asian species, the Indian rhino is found in protected parks in northern India and Nepal; the Sumatran rhino inhabits rain forests from Malaysia to Myanmar (formerly Burma); and the Javan, rarest of all, survives in Indonesia's Udjung Kulon National Park and as a tiny population in Vietnam.

Javan rhinos uproot saplings and spread seeds in their dung, thus helping to regenerate rain forests.

when early rains turn the normally brown, burnt savanna a lush green, rich in vegetation, but less so at the end of winter when drought can have a devastating impact on its food supply.

This tolerance extends to the presence of black rhinos, though such close proximity between the two species is comparatively rare. Black rhinos live in the forests, plains, and scrubland of southern and eastern Africa, browsing for twigs and leaves. They display a remarkable ability to survive in harsh environments such as the Namib Desert in Namibia, southwest Africa.

NO FEAR OF FIRE

Every year, fires spread across vast areas of the African plains. Though these fires serve an important purpose—they destroy the dying undergrowth that prevents new shoots from appearing—they also wreak havoc on local wildlife. The black rhino, however, appears to take it all in its stride, even feeding heartily on the charred remains of acacia scrub. At such times, the black rhino's ability to survive for days without water is crucial.

Indian rhinos, by contrast, are rarely found far from water. Though predominantly grazers, they

Dieter & Mary Plage/Bruce Coleman Ltd.

will supplement their diet of tall elephant grass with the fruits and shrubs that grow around densely thicketed swampland. This is perfect territory for wallowing. The *jheels*, muddy water holes found in northeast India and Nepal, provide one of the few places where the normally antisocial Indian rhinos will tolerate the presence of others—they are the public baths of the rhino world.

> LITTLE IS KNOWN ABOUT THE LIFE OF THE SUMATRAN AND JAVAN RHINOS BECAUSE THEIR REMOTE AND DANGEROUS TERRAIN IS RARELY EXPLORED

Asia's two other species of rhinos, the Javan and the Sumatran, are rarely seen and difficult to study. This is not just because they are rare creatures but also because of their jungle habitat and their secretive nature. Both these timid, elusive species travel alone along well-worn paths through dense rain forest, far from human settlement, browsing for

leaves and fruit and using their enormous weight to break down the young saplings from which they feed. Highly agile, despite their appearance, Sumatran rhinos are found on the steep slopes of mountainous jungle terrain. It is claimed that some have been sighted on the rims of volcanoes, though there appears to be little documented evidence of this. Javan rhinos, on the other hand, prefer to live in swampy lowland rain forests. ■

FOCUS ON

SOUTHERN AFRICAN SCRUB

Between southern Africa's vast savanna and the Namib Desert lies the semiarid scrubland that is home to a small but now-expanding population of black rhinos. Though a relatively inhospitable environment for rhinos, it is one in which man, their chief enemy, is largely absent. The long summers are hot, with temperatures reaching over 86°F (30°C), though it can be bitterly cold at night. Rainfall is infrequent, often as low as 10 inches (250 mm) a year, and evaporates quickly under the intense sun.

For most of the year, the only vegetation consists of woody shrubs that reach about 6.5 feet (2 m) in height. Because these shrubs compete for the small amounts of moisture available, they tend to extend their roots over a wide area. Because food is scarce, the territories of individual rhinos are often large, and this helps to reduce competition between them.

Despite the lack of vegetation, a number of small herbivores such as gerbils manage to survive, as well as grazers like gazelles. These provide prey for carnivores such as leopards and the occasional lion. Creatures commonly associated with desert climates such as lizards and snakes are abundant.

SHARED INTERESTS

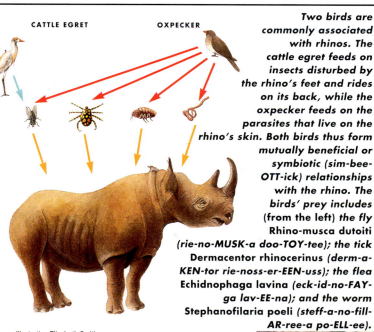

CATTLE EGRET   **OXPECKER**

Two birds are commonly associated with rhinos. The cattle egret feeds on insects disturbed by the rhino's feet and rides on its back, while the oxpecker feeds on the parasites that live on the rhino's skin. Both birds thus form mutually beneficial or symbiotic (sim-bee-OTT-ick) relationships with the rhino. The birds' prey includes (from the left) the fly **Rhino-musca dutoiti** *(rie-no-MUSK-a doo-TOY-tee);* the tick **Dermacentor rhinocerinus** *(derm-a-KEN-tor rie-noss-er-EEN-uss);* the flea **Echidnophaga lavina** *(eck-id-no-FAY-ga lav-EE-na);* and the worm **Stephanofilaria poeli** *(steff-a-no-fill-AR-ree-a po-ELL-ee).*

Illustration Elisabeth Smith

NEIGHBORS

All the creatures featured here share their habitat with the small population of black rhinos that inhabit the harsh semiarid scrubland bordering southern Africa's Namib Desert.

LAPPET-FACED VULTURE

Large scavenging vultures soar above the scrub searching for carrion, which they tear with their strong bills.

GENET

The catlike genet is a solitary hunter and forager, noted for its climbing ability. It makes its home in hollowed-out trees.

Illustrations Elisabeth Smith

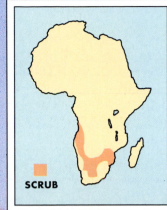

DESERT SCRUB
A great swath of scrub stretches from South Africa's southern Cape Coast through Namibia to Angola. It separates the grasslands and plains of southeast Africa from the Namib in the west and the Kalahari in Botswana and central South Africa.

SCRUB

MODERATELY DANGEROUS

LION
Opportunistic lions will try to ambush young or sick rhinos.

MODERATELY DANGEROUS

SPOTTED HYENA
Packs of hyenas harass rhino mothers and attack their calves.

Illustrations Elisabeth Smith

Clem Haagner/Ardea

COMMON DUIKER

A small, shy antelope that feeds nocturnally, the duiker or "diving buck" is rarely observed in the wild.

SECRETARY BIRD

This ground-hunting bird builds huge nests in thorn trees.

ROBBER FLY

Common throughout sub-Saharan Africa, the robber fly feeds on other insects, which it catches in flight.

LEOPARD TORTOISE

The hard shell of the leopard tortoise presents an almost insoluble problem for any would-be predators.

OXPECKER

Similar in appearance to a starling, the oxpecker spends its time searching for parasites on the rhino's skin.

FOOD AND FEEDING

A large plant-eater, or megaherbivore, like the rhinoceros needs to eat a great deal of plant material in order to maintain its enormous bulk, and most of it is eaten at the beginning and end of the long tropical day. Though rhinos will actively search out the most nutritious leafy plants, their digestive system has adapted to make the most of nutritionally poor foods like twigs and stems.

HIGH-FIBER DIET

Like that of all other ungulates, the rhino's digestive system uses bacteria to help break down cellulose—the fibrous material that strengthens plants—which is very difficult to digest. A small bag called the cecum (SEE-kum), at the end of the small intestine, contains bacteria that ferment the rhino's

THE RHINO'S COMPLEX DIGESTIVE SYSTEM ALLOWS IT TO GAIN NUTRITION FROM THE LEAST PROMISING FOOD SOURCES

food and break down up to half of the cellulose into easily absorbed foods such as sugar.

The rhino's vegetarian diet means that it has no need for sharp incisor teeth. Both African species have lost their front teeth entirely and, even though

inSIGHT

COMMON SENSE

Rhinos have the reputation of being dim of wit as well as vision. This stems from the black rhino's tendency to charge at the first sign of danger and often miss what it should be charging at. To a human—a primate that relies mainly on sight—this seems stupid. But rhinos depend more on hearing and smell than on vision.

Smell is the most important of their senses—the number of olfactory (concerned with smelling) passages in the nose are numerous—and this is the reason why rhinos usually have their nose to the ground. The whole world of the rhino, from its limited social relationships to its voracious appetite for food and its aggressive outbursts, is largely dependent upon the way it "smells" the world.

A JAVAN RHINO

browses through a forest in Southeast Asia, taking advantage of the abundance of leaves and fruit. This species of rhino often breaks down small trees and saplings with its sizable bulk in order to feed on the shoot ends.

Nigel Dennis/NHPA

WHITE RHINOS

have a distinctive square-lipped mouth that is ideal for grazing but less useful for any other kind of feeding. They will suffer if grass is not widely available.

the Asian species have retained theirs, they use them only for fighting. Instead rhinos grind plant material with their back teeth before swallowing.

The lips of the rhino are particularly important for gathering food. Their shape and size give an accurate guide to the feeding habits and food

---

THE WHITE RHINO IS A HIGHLY EFFICIENT GRAZER—RECENT FEEDING GROUNDS TAKE ON THE APPEARANCE OF WELL-KEPT LAWNS

---

preferences of the different species. The white rhino has a very broad, square-lipped mouth, which enables it to take sizable mouthfuls of the short grasses of the savanna, where it spends most of its time grazing. They are such efficient feeders that areas where white rhinos have recently grazed take on the appearance of a freshly mown lawn.

In contrast, the black rhino, which is a browser, has a protruding upper lip that is

prehensile, or adapted for grasping. This enables the rhino to strip branches of their leaves and shoots, thereby increasing its intake of coarse plants, particularly acacia scrub. Indian rhinos share this feature for browsing, though they can fold their upper lip away to graze. They browse most during the winter months, when up to 20 percent of their food intake is made up of the shoots and twigs of low-growing bushes such as mimosa and buffalo thorn. Otherwise, they spend their time in the high elephant grass, eating a variety of crops, water hyacinths, and bamboo shoots. Occasionally they feed on fallen fruit and underground roots.

The other two Asian species, the Sumatran and the Javan, are rain-forest dwellers. They eat fruit, lichen, and fungi. Their intake of fruit is larger than that of the others species. Favorites include figs and mangoes. ■

BROWSERS

like the black rhino are more adaptable in their diet than grazers and are found in harsher semiarid environments, where they survive on shrubs and roots.

Illustrations Dan Wright

SOCIAL STRUCTURE

Rhinos are generally thought of as solitary animals, to the point of being antisocial. Adult males in particular spend most of their time eating and sleeping in isolation from others of their kind, only forming brief associations with females in heat.

What is not readily apparent to the human observer, however, is that the rhino is surrounded by other rhinos, albeit at a distance. All rhinos use scent marks to let other rhinos know they have been there. They may not see each other very often, but rhino society operates by scent rather than sight.

White rhinos are the most sociable species, probably because they live in greater population densities, and occasionally form temporary groups of up to seven animals.

CHANGES IN HABITAT

Female rhinos occupy home ranges, though these differ in size depending on the species and the habitat they occupy. In the open deserts and semiarid land of Namibia in southwest Africa, rhinos may need to cover enormous tracts of land in order to find sufficient food; while in the lush, wet forests of India, rhinos often share small areas.

The ranges of female white and Indian rhinos cover between 3.5 and 6 square miles (9–15 sq km),

---

THE SOCIABILITY OF PARTICULAR RHINO SPECIES IS OFTEN DEPENDENT UPON THEIR HABITAT—THE TOUGHER THE HABITAT, THE LESS SOCIABLE THE RHINO

---

while those of the female black rhino can cover between 1.25 square miles (3 sq km) where there is an abundance of suitable vegetation, and 40 square miles (104 sq km) where the habitat is arid.

White rhino males occupy much larger areas, covering 80 to 250 hectares (200 to 600 acres). When a female in heat enters a dominant male's territory, he attempts to confine her in order to mate; though if the female strays into another breeding male's territory, he will not attempt to follow her.

The males of both African species of rhinos are territorial, although the white is much more so than the black. Males of both species mark their territory by spraying bushes with urine and defecating daily in communal dung heaps that can pile up to 4 feet (1.2 m) high and 20 feet (6 m) across.

Approaching the dung heap, or midden, is something of a ritual: The rhino first smells it, then perhaps prods it with a curious, stiff-legged gait, and then adds to it. To enhance the smell, fresh dung is usually scattered over the midden with powerful backward kicks of the hind legs.

This action also gives the rhino dung-smelling feet, so that wherever it walks it leaves its personal calling card. Any other male who crosses this trail will automatically follow it.

SCENTED STEPS

One scientist tested this behavior by dragging a sack of dung behind his vehicle through the bush. He noted that the trail was followed exactly by rhinos, even where the vehicle had zigzagged. He also found that most rhinos seemed more interested in the scent trails of their own or nearby neighbors' dung than that of total strangers.

As well as the trails of dung, Indian rhinos also leave scent trails produced by glands in their feet. Javan rhinos prefer to spray bushes with their strong-smelling, bright orange urine.

When two rhinos of the same sex meet, they tend to be very wary but may eventually form a temporary association, though this arises from particular feeding and drinking conditions rather

WHITE RHINO BULLS

square up to each other in a confrontation over breeding rights. While violent and sometimes lethal fights do occur, most contests end peacefully when one bull accepts the dominance of the other.

THE RITUAL

wiping of horns on the ground is just one of the gestures performed repeatedly before dominance is conceded.

Illustrations Mathew Hillier/Wildlife Art Agency

than any great desire for social contact. When an outsider enters an area where home ranges have already been established, the newcomer may find itself threatened. Sometimes one of the resident rhinos will charge the intruder. If the stranger retreats, the group will pursue him, though if the intruder shows enough persistence, it may eventually become established in the area.

NO COMPETITION

Breeding males tolerate the presence of subordinate males, but subordinates are not allowed to spray or mark or compete for females. Eventually, though, they may successfully challenge the dominant male and attain his breeding rights.

When breeding males meet on territorial borders, they size each other up for contest. They turn their heads sideways to impress with the size of their horns, then go through some ritual fencing. Sometimes fights break out, with the opponents jabbing one another with their horns. More often, confrontations end with the two males happy to return to the heart of their respective territories. ■

in SIGHT

VOCALIZATIONS

Rhinos communicate with a wide range of calls, though their exact meaning is not always clear. Females and calves keep in touch with soft, high-pitched sounds (similar to a cow's mooing sound). Louder squeals are used as a contact call. Males use a series of deeper grunts, snorts, and bellows, particularly when courting. Female Indian rhinos give a strange whistle each time they breathe to let any males know they are ready to mate.

THREATENED

white rhinos press their tails together and face outwards to form a defensive formation.

Frans Lanting/ZEFA-Minden

LIFE CYCLE

Rhinos live long lives, maturing slowly and progressing steadily through life's stages. The rearing of young is no exception.

The rituals of rhino courtship are prolonged, complicated, and sometimes violent, none more so than that of the Indian species. The female will ward off the approaching bull with a charge, slashing her sharp incisor teeth at him. Only when she has fought with him to the point of exhaustion will mating take place.

CONFLICTING INTERESTS

Rhinos commonly spend more than an hour mating, during which time the male is mounted on the female's back. Rhino males are renowned for their astonishing sexual staying powers—probably the source of the mythical aphrodisiac power of the rhino's horn. By this time, the cow seems surprisingly unconcerned, walking around and feeding while the bull tries to maintain the coupling.

MATING BETWEEN RHINOS IS PROLONGED, AND THIS MAY HAVE LED TO THE MYTH THAT THE HUMAN MALE CAN IMPROVE HIS SEXUAL PROWESS WITH RHINO HORN

Rhinos rarely give birth to more than one calf—only white rhino twins have been observed. Births take place at any time of the year, but, for African rhinos at least, the peak is reached at the beginning of the dry season.

The prospective mother usually finds some dense cover in which to give birth, always keeping a sharp ear and nose out for lions or hyenas if it is an

NEWBORN
rhinos are at the most risk from predators, even though they can get to their feet almost immediately.

SNIFFING IN
the scent of a female's urine, the male rhino can gather information about her sexual receptivity.

Illustrations John Cox/Wildlife Art Agency

PLAYTIME
often involves mother and baby rubbing their horns together.

in SIGHT

BORN LEADERS

Black rhino calves run behind their mothers, whereas the young of the white rhino tend to trot along a few steps ahead. This is thought to be because of habitat differences: A black rhino predator usually hides in ambush, so the mother will meet it first, while, in more open grasslands, predators such as hyenas are likely to chase prey from behind.

Mark Boulton/ICCE Photo Library

GROWING UP

The life of a young black rhino

THE YOUNG CALF

will continue to suckle its mother's milk for about eighteen months, though it will start to eat grasses and leaves when it is a few weeks old.

KEEPING CLOSE

to its mother, a baby black rhino will follow a few paces behind when accompanying her on her travels.

FROM BIRTH TO DEATH

BLACK RHINO
GESTATION: 15 MONTHS
LITTER SIZE: 1
BIRTH INTERVAL: 3 YEARS
WEIGHT AT BIRTH: 48–100 LB
(22–45 KG)

WEANING: 18 MONTHS
INDEPENDENCE: 2–3 YEARS
SEXUAL MATURITY: FEMALES
4–5 YEARS, MALES 6–7 YEARS
LONGEVITY: 40 YEARS

WHITE RHINO
GESTATION: 16 MONTHS
LITTER SIZE: USUALLY 1, BUT
OCCASIONALLY 2
BIRTH INTERVAL: 4 YEARS
WEIGHT AT BIRTH: 185 LB (84 KG)

WEANING: BETWEEN 1 AND 2
YEARS
INDEPENDENCE: 2–3 YEARS
SEXUAL MATURITY: FEMALES
4–5 YEARS, MALES 6–7 YEARS
LONGEVITY: 45 YEARS

INDIAN RHINO
GESTATION: 16 MONTHS
LITTER SIZE: 1
BIRTH INTERVAL: 3 YEARS
WEIGHT AT BIRTH: 120–145 LB
(54–66 KG)

WEANING: NOT KNOWN IN
WILD
INDEPENDENCE: 2–3 YEARS?
SEXUAL MATURITY: FEMALES
5 YEARS, MALES 7–9 YEARS
LONGEVITY: 45–50 YEARS

African species, tigers if it is Asian.

The newborn baby's weight will be about 4 percent of its mother's, which differs among the species. For the first couple of days the mother suckles the calf every hour or two, but the calf only sucks for two to three minutes at a time. As it gains strength, the

> A CALF WILL STAY WITH ITS MOTHER UNTIL A NEW CALF IS BORN, OR FOR UP TO FOUR YEARS. A CLOSE BOND DEVELOPS BETWEEN THEM DURING THIS TIME

feeding bouts become longer and less frequent. The young calf will drink up to 35 pints (17 liters) of its mother's rich milk every day.

Black rhino calves may nibble at solid foods at only nine days old and will supplement their mother's milk regularly after one month. White rhino calves don't try their first grass until they are about two months old. Though they are weaned at about eighteen months, youngsters will not usually become independent until they are two or three years old.

LATE DEVELOPERS

Female African rhinos reach sexual maturity after four or five year, and will have their first calf by the age of six or seven. Though they are sexually mature at seven or eight, males are unlikely to breed until they have proved themselves in combat with older males. This rarely happens before they are at least ten years of age. This is not a problem, however, since rhinos can live for up to forty years. ■

On the Brink of Extinction

Highly prized for centuries in the Far East for its medicinal powers, the rhino's horn—its only defensive weapon—may, ironically, seal its fate

D OOMED—to disappear from the face of the earth due to man's folly, greed, neglect . . . ," screamed the front-page headline over a picture of a mother and baby black rhino. *The Daily Mirror* of October 9, 1961, carried this dire warning in a special "shock issue" to mark the launch of the World Wide Fund for Nature (WWF). The paper warned that, unless its readers responded, the phrase "dead as a dodo" could be replaced by "dead as a rhino."

TOUCHING HEARTS

The appeal was a great success, bringing in a flood of donations, and the WWF went on to become the largest nongovernmental conservation organization in the world. Sadly, the rhino mother that had been featured in the paper—a famous resident of Kenya's Amboseli National Park known as "Gertie"—was killed by poachers a few years later.

THE WORLD WIDE FUND FOR NATURE HAS PLAYED AN IMPORTANT ROLE IN BRINGING THE PLIGHT OF THE RHINO TO THE PUBLIC'S ATTENTION

The reasons for rhino poaching are often misunderstood. There is a widespread myth, often repeated in news reports, that rhino horn is an aphrodisiac, particularly in China. This is not strictly true.

The Chinese do use all sorts of unusual animal parts as aphrodisiacs, but rhino horn is not one of them. There is a small demand for rhino horn aphrodisiacs in northern India, but this has never been a major destination for poached horn. There are two main markets for it, though, both steeped in tradition, and both booming as a result of a sudden rise in standards of living.

Rhino horn and other body parts have been used in traditional Eastern medicine for thousands of years, and the horn's high value is largely due to the faith that people have in its supposed curative effect. Sometimes the horn is powdered, sometimes thin shavings are boiled with herbs, sometimes it is mixed with other ingredients to make tea balls— wax-coated pills the size of marbles that are dissolved in hot tea.

Such remedies are prescribed for an astonishing variety of ailments. The Chinese *Materia Medica* lists rhino horn as an antidote to poisons and as a cure for possession by devils, hallucinations, nightmares, infantile convulsions, and dysentery; it is claimed to calm the liver, clear the vision, and treat typhoid, headaches, feverish colds, and numerous other complaints. The key question, though, is: Does it work?

To combat poaching, a vet darts a black rhino from the air (right) *in order to dehorn it. Rhino horn is widely used in Chinese medicines* (above).

Emma Lee/Life-File

Anthony Bannister/NHPA

The map below shows the former and current distribution of the black rhino.

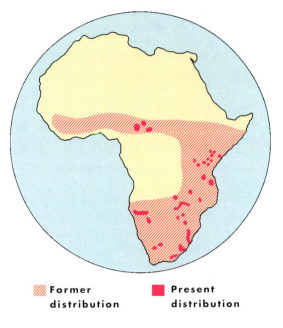

▨ **Former distribution**   ■ **Present distribution**

The chart below shows black rhino population trends in Africa. Severe losses have occurred in Tanzania and in the Central African Republic, where the black rhino may have died out completely. Zimbabwe's once stable population has fallen since 1986 because wildlife protection policies are underfunded. Kenyan sanctuaries, however, have halted the decline in their black rhino numbers.

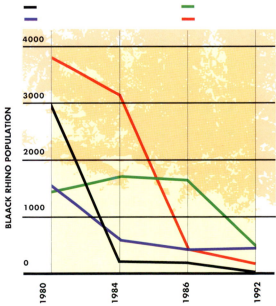

Laboratory tests have failed to show any positive results, except in one case where a highly concentrated solution was found to lower the temperature of feverish rats slightly. At best, this effect was comparable to an aspirin, and for those who prefer a traditional alternative, water-buffalo horn was found to have a similar effect. This suggests that rhino-horn medicines are almost completely ineffective, and that users are motivated by factors such as tradition, prestige, and faith rather than by a lack of alternatives.

NEWFOUND WEALTH

Rhino horn has always been expensive, but, with the economic boom in Southeast Asia, an increasing number of people can afford to buy it and there has been a huge and lucrative market. Prices are highest in Taiwan, where African rhino horns have retailed for thousands of dollars per kilo, and Asian horns (which are considered much more powerful) at even more. Despite laws against the trade, it goes on openly in the capital, Taipei, and this has led conservation groups to call for boycotts of goods made in Taiwan, as well as those of the other major consumers, China, Hong Kong, and South Korea.

The second traditional use for rhino horn is for the ornate dagger handles of Yemen in southern Arabia. When a Yemeni boy comes of age, he is presented with a carved ceremonial dagger called a *jambia* by his father. This *jambia* is worn tucked in his belt as a symbol of his manhood, and every

OPERATION STRONGHOLD

In 1984, a new plan called Operation Stronghold was launched to combat the poachers crossing the borders of the Zambezi Valley between Zambia and Zimbabwe's Gonarhezhou National Park.

Before 1985, the rangers were not allowed to shoot poachers. Since then, more than 150 poachers have been shot and many more arrested, though 50 game rangers have also lost their lives.

In addition, the plan included transporting rhinos from high-risk border areas to regions of low (or lower) risk in the middle of the country.

Despite these efforts, poaching has continued. In 1991, a dehorning policy was introduced as a last-ditch attempt to deter the poachers, but even hornless rhinos are now being killed.

Alain Compost/Bruce Coleman Ltd.

THE JAVAN RHINO: IN THE SHADOW OF KRAKATOA

Krakatoa

Java

Few people have ever seen a Javan rhino in the wild. The only way scientists can find out about this elusive species is to study its tracks, or to trap one alive and attach a radio collar so that its movements can be monitored when it is released. This kind of research is vital because conservationists must understand its ecological needs to ensure its survival.

DWINDLING NUMBERS

The Javan rhinoceros has the smallest population of any endangered large mammal species, found only in two small areas of rain forest—one in Java and one in Vietnam. There are none in captivity.

Most Javan rhinos live in Ujung Kulon National Park, a swampy, rain-forested peninsula on the westernmost tip of the island of Java. At its lowest ebb, in 1970, this population was thought to number only 30 animals. By 1980 the estimate was 55, and the number has remained stable ever since, with the 1992 estimate being 55 to 75. Until 1988, these were thought to be the only surviving Javan rhinos. In that year, however, a hunter killed a rhino in the Lan Dong province of

Alain Compost/Bruce Coleman Ltd.

FOR NOW AT LEAST, THE JAVAN RHINO IS THRIVING IN UJUNG KULON NATIONAL PARK.

CONSERVATION MEASURES

With so many threats facing the Javan rhino, the success of any conservation effort seems doubtful.

● There are plans to move some of the Ujung Kulon rhinos to another location, such as the nearby Way Kambas National Park in Sumatra, so that they may be at a

southern Vietnam. Its skeleton was sent to Hanoi and the existence of this second population was accepted. Subsequent surveys have revealed an estimate of 8 to 12 rhinos in Vietnam.

The discovery of a second population is of great importance because of two catastrophic risks: volcanoes and disease. Ujung Kulon is close to the volcanic island of Krakatoa, which blew in 1883 in one of the biggest eruptions on record. If this were to happen again, Ujung Kulon would be covered in volcanic ash. After the 1883 eruption, the forest there slowly regenerated and the rhinos were able to recolonize the peninsula from the surrounding forest. Now, though, there is no surrounding forest to act as a temporary refuge for the rhinos.

The risk of a fatal epidemic is also very real. In 1982, several Javan rhinos died of an epidemic and, although the population recovered, it served as a clear warning. With fewer than eighty of these animals left in the world, can we risk losing even one individual?

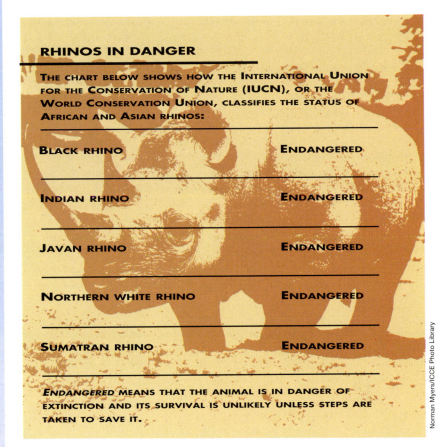

RHINOS IN DANGER

THE CHART BELOW SHOWS HOW THE INTERNATIONAL UNION FOR THE CONSERVATION OF NATURE (IUCN), OR THE WORLD CONSERVATION UNION, CLASSIFIES THE STATUS OF AFRICAN AND ASIAN RHINOS:

BLACK RHINO	ENDANGERED
INDIAN RHINO	ENDANGERED
JAVAN RHINO	ENDANGERED
NORTHERN WHITE RHINO	ENDANGERED
SUMATRAN RHINO	ENDANGERED

ENDANGERED MEANS THAT THE ANIMAL IS IN DANGER OF EXTINCTION AND ITS SURVIVAL IS UNLIKELY UNLESS STEPS ARE TAKEN TO SAVE IT.

Norman Myers/ICCE Photo Library

safe distance if Krakatoa erupts.

● A proposal has been made to establish a captive population, but critics point out that no zoo has successfully bred Javan rhinos in the past, and that similar attempts to save the Sumatran rhino have yet to succeed.

ENDANGERED SPECIES

father wishes to give his son the finest *jambia* he can afford. In the past, only the richest princes and noblemen could afford a rhino-horn dagger. Everyone else made do with wood or cow horn, but these tend to become tatty with age, whereas a rhino-horn handle actually improves as it ages.

In the 1970s, many Yemeni men went to work in the nearby Saudi Arabian oil fields and, when they returned home with bulging wallets, they bought the finest gift a father could give his son. As a result, the demand for rhino-horn handles shot up, and Yemen became a major horn importer. It also became an exporter, because the shavings left over

WITH A RISE IN THE STANDARD OF LIVING IN YEMEN, MORE AND MORE PEOPLE CAN AFFORD TO BUY RHINO-HORN HANDLES FOR THEIR TRADITIONAL DAGGERS

from carving the handles were then shipped to the Far East for use in traditional medicines.

During the 1970s, the main merchant in Yemen was carving 6,000 dagger handles a year, all of them rhino horn. Imports were banned in 1982 in response to appeals from conservationists, but in 1986 he was still carving 2,400 rhino-horn handles a year, although this now represented only 10

A L O N G S I D E M A N

WHAT CAN A ZOO DO?

The arguments for and against zoos are well illustrated by two species of rhino. Operation Rhino was a bold plan by the Natal Parks Board in South Africa to send "surplus" white rhinos to zoos. Whipsnade Zoo Park in England received twenty in August 1970, and by 1993 thirty-nine calves had been born, many of which have been sent to other zoos. Even if the poachers do their worst in Africa, the subspecies is now considered safe from extinction.

Sumatran rhinos have not fared as well in zoos. Between 1984 and 1991, American zoos captured thirty-two Sumatran rhinos to establish a captive breeding population. Nine of them died during or soon after shipment, and no births have yet been reported. Zoos have had a long history of caring for white rhinos, but most of what was learned about Sumatran rhino husbandry has been learned since 1984.

Whipsnade Zoo

percent of his total output. Between 1970 and 1990, this merchant used a total of almost 80,000 pounds (36,000 kg) of horn, which represents the death of as many as 13,000 black rhinos.

A LOSING BATTLE

It seems that the writing has been on the wall for rhinos for some time. In 1961 Sir Peter Scott, one of the founders of World Wide Fund for Nature, predicted on television that the black rhinoceros would be extinct in thirty years. Despite the best efforts of conservationists, the shoot-outs with poachers and the televised exposés of dealers, the decline in rhino populations continues.

In Kenya, for example, numbers of black rhinos fell from a total of 19,000 in 1970 to fewer than 400 in 1987, which amounts to a loss of 98 percent of

White rhinos graze peacefully at Whipsnade Zoo Park, England (above right).

A jambia seller in Yemen displays his collection of rhino-horn daggers.

the population in just seventeen years. In Africa as a whole, numbers of black rhinos were drastically reduced from 8,800 animals in 1984 to 3,380 in 1987. It may have been a little premature, but Sir Peter's prediction could yet come about.

The largest and most successful conservation treaty, CITES (Convention on International Trade in Endangered Species), seems to have failed the rhinos. The Asian species were listed on Appendix I (which bans trade) in 1975, when the treaty first came into force. Both African species were added in 1977, so commercial imports and exports of rhino horn, carvings, or medicines have been illegal in all member countries since then. But the trade has continued, and many of the smuggling routes lead to Taiwan.

Taiwan is not recognized as a country by the United Nations because it is claimed by China, so it cannot join CITES, but it has passed its own laws prohibiting imports of rhino horn. Until recently,

> AS A RESULT OF THE INTERNATIONAL BOYCOTT ON GOODS MADE IN TAIWAN, TRADERS CAN NO LONGER IGNORE THE BAN ON RHINO-HORN IMPORTS

the Taiwan authorities were not effectively enforcing the law against rhino-horn trade. In 1993, as a result of political pressure, the threat of sanctions by the United States and CITES, and a consumer boycott of goods made in Taiwan, the rhino-horn traders were finally forced to obey the law. It remains to be seen, however, whether this will affect the poaching in Africa and Asia. ∎

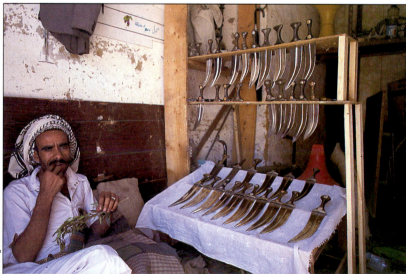

Juliet Highet/Life-File

INTO THE FUTURE

Although the future for rhinos looks bleak, there is room for optimism. In a few countries, the fall in rhino numbers has been stemmed, and modest increases are being reported. The key factor is money: If the politicians give their wildlife departments enough money, or if private sources can be found to finance the work, rhinos can be saved.

Protection costs are often expressed in terms of how many U.S. dollars per square mile must be spent each year. In Zimbabwe, protecting each square mile of black rhino habitat costs $1,040 per year, which allows for one ranger per twenty to fifty square miles, including aircraft, vehicles, and equipment. In 1991, it cost only $143 per square mile to protect Garamba National Park in Zaire, where the last northern white rhinos have increased from fifteen survivors in 1984 to thirty-one in 1992.

Morale is another factor. In Zimbabwe, for example, game rangers are paid about one dollar a day to put their life on the line against well-armed poachers. In 1993, the Zimbabwe wildlife department was so underfunded that it was unable to patrol the parks for four months.

Rhino sanctuaries, as pioneered by Kenya, have

PREDICTION

NORTHERN WHITE RHINO

If the protection of Zaire's Garamba National Park continues to be so successful, the northern white rhinoceros population there may have a good chance of following the southern white rhino on the road to recovery.

proved highly successful in protecting the black rhino. Instead of trying to patrol huge areas of wilderness, Kenyan rhinos were moved into relatively small, fenced areas of suitable habitat.

The advantages to this are twofold: First, by concentrating manpower and resources into a small area, the poachers can be kept at bay. Second, it is easier for the rhinos to find each other to mate, so the birth rate goes up. As numbers rise, the fenced areas are enlarged, or a number of rhinos might be moved to repopulate areas where the species was once found. Eventually, all the parks using this method should be able to maintain a healthy population of black rhinos once again. ∎

A SECOND CHANCE

At the 1992 CITES meeting, five southern African states—including Zimbabwe, South Africa, and Namibia—made a proposal to reopen the trade in rhino horn. They argued that the stocks of horn in their storerooms should be sold to raise money for their conservation work. The proposal was withdrawn when virtually every other country argued against it, and the trade in rhino horns has not been reopened since. The United Nations Special Envoy for Rhinos, Dr. Esmond Bradley Martin, argues that now, when rhino numbers are so low and only four countries are major consumers, is not the time to begin marketing legal rhino horn. The pro-trade lobby points out that trade bans have not worked, and so something radical and new is called for. Either way, some fear poaching is destined to continue until the last rhino is dead.

DEHORNING RHINOS

The idea to remove the horns from rhinos to protect them from poachers was first discussed in Africa in the 1950s, but it was not until 1989 that it was first tried, because many scientists were worried that the rhinos would have less chance of surviving without their main defensive weapon.

In mid-1989, just after six rare, desert-dwelling rhinos were poached in Damaraland, Namibia, the decision was taken to dehorn the rhinos most at risk. No ill effects were seen in the careful follow-up study, so Zimbabwe soon followed Namibia's example and, since 1991, all translocated rhinos in Zimbabwe have been dehorned. Each time a rhino is darted and the horn cut off, it costs around $1,000, but it is considered worth it.

Sadly, in 1993, even dehorned rhinos were being shot in Zimbabwe, and of the eighty-five white rhino dehorned in Hwange National Park in 1991–92, only two had survived by mid-1993. Some conservationists fear that a trader with a large stock of horn is trying to kill all the rhinos so that his horn will increase in value—literally banking on the rhino's extinction. If that is the case, the only thing that can save the rhino is if the consumers stop buying rhino horn. It would then become worthless, and the economic incentive to wipe out the rhinos would disappear.

Illustration John Morris/Wildlife Art Agency

EARED SEALS

Seals and the walrus are members of the order known as the Pinnipedia. Other members of the order include:

WALRUS

TRUE SEALS

CALIFORNIA SEA LION

STELLER SEA LION

SOUTHERN SEA LION

Georgette Douwma/Planet Earth Pictures

Eared seals, true seals, and the walrus all belong to the order Pinnipedia. Each group has a separate subfamily. So-called sea lions are actually eared seals.

ORDER

Pinnipedia

FAMILIES

Otariidae

Odobenidae

SPECIES

There are fourteen species in seven genera

GENERA

Callorhinus
(northern fur seal)

Arctocephalus
(southern fur seal)

Eumetopias
(Steller sea lion)

Zalophus
(California sea lion)

Otaria
(southern sea lion)

Neophoca
(Australian sea lion)

Phocarctos
(Auckland sea lion)

Odobenus
(walruses)

GRACEFUL SWIMMERS

THE EARED SEALS AND WALRUS SPEND
MOST OF THEIR TIME HUNTING IN THEIR OCEAN ENVIRONMENT,
COMING TO LAND ONLY TO REST, MATE, AND GIVE BIRTH

The world of seals is divided between the true seals, the phocids (FOKE-ids), and the eared seals, the otariids (o-tar-EYE-ids), which include fur seals and sea lions. Although members of these two families look superficially alike—both have a streamlined body shape and use flippers to propel themselves—there are many differences between them that suggest that they are not very closely related and that they are the descendants of different ancestors.

The fur seals and sea lions seem to have arisen from the same land animal that gave rise to dogs and bears, while the true seals are probably descended from an aquatic weasel. It was thought that the true seals (called "true" because they were the first to be named) developed on the shores of the northern Atlantic. Eared seals were believed to have evolved in the North Pacific. However, new paleontological and molecular evidence has upset the old theories, and now it looks as though eared

seals and true seals are descended from the same aquatic mammals in the North Pacific. The first true otariids appeared about 12 million years ago, but they did not begin to diversify into their modern forms until 3 million years ago. New evidence suggests that the walrus is so closely related to seals, it should really be regarded as one.

Seals are classified primarily on the basis of whether or not their ears are visible. Other anatomical differences exist under the blubber, but the ears provide an instant clue to identification. However, the ears are not very big, even on

---

SEALS POSSESS A THICK LAYER OF FAT BENEATH THE SKIN, CALLED BLUBBER, WHICH KEEPS THEM WARM

---

fur seals and sea lions. California sea lions' ears are only 2.5 in (6 cm) long and shaped unobtrusively like scrolls. True seals have only small oval holes, which close underwater.

Eared seals and true seals differ in the way they move as well as how they appear. Both have webbed flippers like paddles, which can be used independently, but eared seals scull themselves through the water using their front flippers, while true seals use their tail flippers for propulsion. On land, eared seals can turn their hind flippers forward and use all four limbs for walking. True seals are far less agile. They "hump" along the beach on

E. Mickleburgh/Ardea

An adult Antarctic fur seal lifts its head and calls to its young. Seals have acute hearing.

FUR SEALS AND SEA LIONS

Dieter and Mary Plage/Survival Anglia

There are a few differences between fur seals and sea lions. Sea lions have blunt noses and their coats are quite thin. Fur seals have sharp noses and their coats are thick. Most sea lions are larger than fur seals. Despite these cosmetic differences, fur seals and sea lions are very closely related. In nearly all species of both sea lions and seals, males are larger than females. This means they are able to catch different prey and, in effect, the two sexes occupy separate niches in the food web, rather than competing with each other.

their bellies, in caterpillar fashion. Their forelimbs are too small to be of any use for walking, and they cannot prop themselves up in order to look around in the typical style of eared seals. These differences allow eared seals to breed a short distance inland, if they wish, while true seals tend to stay close to the water at all times. Although eared seals are much more agile than true seals on land, the differences between them are less pronounced in the sea, where their bodies are supported by water.

There are several other small differences. Lying below the thick soft fur of their undercoat, the skin of fur seals is light-colored, not black. The nails on the first three "fingers" of their flippers are longer than the other two, and the "palms" of the flippers are hairless. Eared seal females have four nipples,

James A. Rowan/Tony Stone Worldwide

California sea lions lie back on the rocks, enjoying the warmth of the sun on their bodies.

while true seals sometimes have only two.

Whether or not eared seals and true seals share the same ancestors, they have evolved with the same constraints. They share many features because they have had the same problems to overcome. Warm-blooded mammals quickly suffer from exposure in the sea because water conducts heat much more efficiently than air. The bodies of eared seals and true seals are streamlined and cushioned by a layer of blubber—a dense form of fat that acts not only as a food store, but also as a thermal vest. The sea is not only cold, but dark, which makes it hard to find food. Both families of seals have evolved large eyes and excellent hearing. Their long whiskers act as antennae to pick up the underwater vibrations of small fish and crustaceans.

Seals inhabit every sea in the world and are found along every coast of every continent. They have adapted to the coldest waters of our planet, as well as to the warmest. However, eared seals are found only in the open sea, never in bays or freshwater inlets, while some species of true seals migrate up rivers or even live in lakes.

The ability to swim gives seals the power to hunt over huge areas of ocean. They use tides and currents to their advantage, enabling them to travel much farther than most land-based predators. ∎

THE SEALS' FAMILY TREE

The family tree shows the relationship between the eared seals and the one remaining species of walrus. Eared seals belong to the family Otariidae, and within this there are seven genera containing fourteen different species with some subspecies. The walrus belongs to the family Odobenidae, of which it is the only living member.

NORTHERN FUR SEAL
Callorhinus ursinus
(ka-lor-HINE-us UR-sin-us)

Inhabitants of the North Pacific, males are generally darker than females. They are almost twice the size and may weigh five times as much. It is the only species in its genus.

ANCESTORS

At one time, besides the eared and true seals, there were two other groups of marine carnivores: the Enaliarctidae and Desmatophocidae, both of which became extinct. Members of the Enaliarctidae were thought to be coastal-dwellers, found off the coast of California. They gave rise to the Desmatophocids, which are said to be the link to today's eared seals. They are also known from off the coast of California, as well as Oregon and farther up the western seaboard, and also Japan.

A little later, a walrus-sized mammal, called Imagotaria, appeared. By the end of the Miocene period (five million years ago), there were at least five genera of walrus on the North Pacific coast.

OTHER EARED SEALS:
NORTHERN, OR STELLER, SEA LION—
SOUTHERN, OR SOUTH AMERICAN,
SEA LION
AUSTRALIAN SEA LION
HOOKER'S, NEW ZEALAND, OR
AUCKLAND, SEA LION
EIGHT SPECIES OF
SOUTHERN FUR SEALS—GENUS
ARCTOCEPHALUS

ENALIARCTOS
Enaliarctos

IMAGOTARIA
Imagotaria

CALIFORNIA SEA LION
Zalophus Californianus
(ZALL-o-fuss kal-ee-for-nee-AN-us)

The sleek California sea lion is a coastal animal that likes to haul out on shore any time of the year. The sturdy males are usually a darker brown than the smaller females. Males have an extremely prominent forehead. This seal is considered to be one of the most playful of all.

SUBSPECIES

THERE ARE THREE RECOGNIZED, ISOLATED SUBSPECIES:
Z. C. CALIFORNIANUS—
(PACIFIC COAST OF NORTH AMERICA)
Z. C. JAPONICUS—
(JAPAN AND KOREA)
Z. C. WOLLEBAKEI—
(GALAPAGOS ISLANDS)

WALRUS
Odobenus rosmarus
(odd-o-BEN-us ROSE-ma-rus)

SUBSPECIES

ATLANTIC WALRUS
PACIFIC WALRUS

EARED SEALS

TRUE SEALS

The walrus is primarily found in the coastal waters of the Arctic Ocean and adjoining seas. Males are enormous—up to 11.5 ft (3.5 m) long and 3,750 lb (1,700 kg) in weight. The long tusks are a well-known feature of the adult animals.

EARED SEALS
AND WALRUS

ALL SEALS

A N A T O M Y:
THE FUR SEALS

Eared seals (front) vary in length from 4–11.5 ft (120–350 cm) with the males usually being considerably larger and heavier than the females. At a length of 9–11.7 ft (275–355 cm), the walrus can be considerably larger.

NOSE
Everything about the seal is stream-lined to make it effective in the water. Even the nostrils are narrow slits that can be closed when swimming.

FRONT FLIPPERS
Front flippers are used for powering the seal in the water.

HIND FLIPPERS
The elongated digits of the hind flippers are clearly visible. The fact that they are slightly splayed helps give the seals some traction when they lumber across land. They are also able to turn these flippers forward, which makes them more effective in pushing them along.

WALRUS SKULL

14-inch-long skull

Tusk

Robin Budden/Wildlife Art Agency

WALRUS
The famous walrus tusks are actually the upper canine teeth, which grow throughout a walrus's life. They can grow to 22 in (55 cm) long in males and 16 in (40 cm) in females. Females' tusks are more slender and bend farther backward. They are mainly used to help pull the large body out of the water.

X RAY

The skeleton of eared seals reflectss both their swimming ability and their maneuverability on dry land. Vertebrae of the neck are enlarged to support powerful muscles used for swimming.

FUR SEAL SKELETON

FUR SEAL SKULL (side view)

canine teeth

The flattened skull of an eared seal. The cheek teeth are simple and peglike and tend to drop out in advancing years.

X-ray illustrations Elisabeth Smith

EAR
Even though the ear is visible, it is very small.

EYES
The large round eyes give clear vision both in and out of the water. The retina is adapted for the low light conditions usually found underwater.

Robin Budden/Wildlife Art Agency

Robin Budden/Wildlife Art Agency

FACT FILE:
NORTHERN FUR SEAL

CLASSIFICATION
GENUS: *CALLORHINUS*
SPECIES: *URSINUS*

SIZE
HEAD-TAIL LENGTH/MALE: 84 IN (213 CM)
HEAD-TAIL LENGTH/FEMALE: 56 IN (142 CM)
WEIGHT/MALE: 397–529 LB (180–240 KG)
WEIGHT/FEMALE: 95–110 LB (43–50 KG)

COLORATION
APPEARS VERY DARK OR BLACK WHEN THE COAT IS WET, BUT VARIOUS SHADES OF BROWN WHEN COAT IS DRY

WALRUS

CLASSIFICATION
GENUS: *ODOBENUS*
SPECIES: *ROSMARUS*
SOLE MEMBER OF GENUS

SIZE
HEAD-TAIL/MALE: 8.8–11.7 FT (268–356 CM)
HEAD-TAIL/FEMALE: 7.4–10.2 FT (226–311 CM)
WEIGHT/MALE: 1,764–3,748 LB (800–1,700 KG)
WEIGHT/FEMALE: 882–2,755 LB (400–1,250 KG)
TUSK LENGTH/MALE: 14–22 IN (36–56 CM)
TUSK LENGTH/FEMALE: 9–16 IN (23–41 CM)

COLORATION
FROM PALE TAWNY TO REDDISH BROWN. IMMATURE ANIMALS ARE DARKER THAN ADULTS
COAT IS DARKER ON UNDERSIDE
HAIRLESS SURFACES OF FLIPPERS ARE BLACK IN YOUNG ANIMALS, TURNING TO BROWN OR GRAY WITH AGE

FRONT FLIPPER
The digits (fingers) are greatly elongated in forelimbs (seen here).

large shoulder blades

sturdy elbows

long digits

GUARD HAIR

PELT SECTION

Long guard hairs are interspersed through the coat with shorter, finer hairs, which comprise a dense covering of underfur. The fur is water-repellent and acts as insulation.

MARINE HUNTERS

ALTHOUGH THEY MAY APPEAR TO BE CLUMSY ON LAND, SEA LIONS AND FUR SEALS ARE THE BALLERINAS AND ACROBATS OF THE OCEANS

T he California sea lion is the circus favorite, performing amazing feats of balance and coordination with colored balls and hoops. All seals are playful, but sea lions seem to be the most naturally exuberant of all. They are often seen body-surfing the California waves, chasing one another in wild games of tag, turning somersaults, and pursuing their own bubbles.

Sea lions are gregarious and like to form "rafts," floating together in the water in groups many hundred strong. They drift along until suddenly, with

Cape fur seals (right) are closer to the sea lions than to other fur seals. They haul out to mate and give birth on the beaches of South Africa from October to January.

John Waters/Planet Earth Pictures

no signal and for no apparent reason, they all dive beneath the water together.

Fur seals are less friendly with one another. Most species lead solitary lives outside the breeding season, and it is unusual to see two together when they are fishing. These seals spend long periods of time far out in the ocean, resting and sleeping in the water in between bouts of diving for prey. However, they form extraordinarily dense

South American sea lions (above) are the most lionlike of all. They are found from the coast of Brazil, around the southern tip of South America, to Peru.

The northern fur seal lives in the cold waters of the Bering Sea. It is often called the Alaskan seal.

Kenneth W. Fink/Ardea

congregations on land during the breeding season.

Seals need the protection of numbers while they are giving birth, for young seals figure on the menu of a wide range of predators, from gulls to sharks. If all the pups are born around the same time, the predators are overwhelmed by sheer numbers and a higher percentage of young seals survive. It is a strategy that works, but a closer look at a seal colony shows that seals are not naturally "social" animals. They do not form close friendly bonds with one another, except (temporarily) with their

---

IN VERY HOT WEATHER SEALS FAN THEIR FLIPPERS TO LOSE HEAT ACROSS THEIR BODIES

---

own young. Each animal acts independently, for its own benefit. They may be packed tightly together on the breeding beach, but there is no sense of caring cooperation in a seal colony. Males seldom take any interest in pups; instead they are far more concerned with fighting each other, and they often inadvertently squash the newborn seals as they lumber around defending their territory. Females are continually bickering among themselves, flapping their flippers at one another and sometimes even biting neighboring pups that come too close. They need the security of numbers, but they hate being in such close proximity to each other! ■

Clem Haagner/Ardea

HABITATS

Although the eared seals originated in the North Pacific, they have diversified most successfully in the south. Six species of fur seals and three families of sea lions are found in the Southern Hemisphere, while only two kinds of fur seals and two families of sea lions remain in the north. A subspecies of the California sea lion, the Galápagos sea lion, breeds right at the equator, along with the Galapagos fur seal.

People tend to link seals with the place where they come on land to breed. The Juan Fernandez fur seals, for example, will be forever associated with the islands of that name off the Chilean coast, although, in fact, these oceangoing seals may hunt over a wider area of the eastern Pacific. All fur seals were exploited for their fur soon after their discovery in the 17th and 18th centuries, so their modern distribution reflects not their love for small islands, but the fact that it was only in the most remote places that they survived.

Besides the Pacific coast of North America and the Galápagos Islands, California sea lions were once also found off the coasts of Korea and Japan. They are more shore-loving than other fur seals and are seldom seen far out in the ocean.

A double coat of thick underfur covered by guard hairs enables fur seals to withstand the cold. A layer of blubber completes the insulation, keeping Antarctic fur seals warm in the bitterest weather. They breed on islands such as South Georgia and Kerguelen in December, at the beginning of the austral summer. The newborn seal leaves the warmth of its mother's body for an icy,

A playful New Zealand sea lion riding the bow waves around Campbell Island.

Antarctic fur seal bull enjoying a scratch. This seal's fur is one of the densest.

Ben Osborne/Oxford Scientific Films

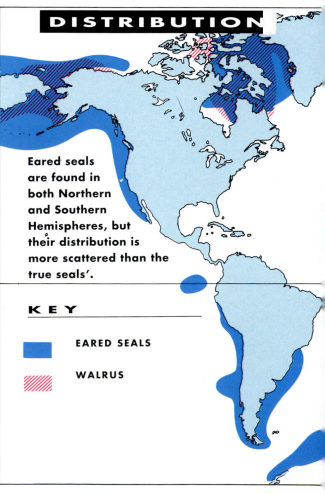

DISTRIBUTION

Eared seals are found in both Northern and Southern Hemispheres, but their distribution is more scattered than the true seals'.

KEY

■ EARED SEALS

▨ WALRUS

Kim Westerskov/Oxford Scientific Films

windswept world—a temperature drop of perhaps 38°F (21°C). Like other fur seals born into harsh conditions, the Antarctic fur seal is forced to become independent in only four months.

Most of the world's population of subantarctic seals breed on Gough Island, about 1,426 miles (2,300 km) southeast of Cape Town. It is warmer here and mothers are able to nurse their offspring for eleven months, until the next pup is born. These

---

THE SEBACEOUS GLANDS OF THE FUR SEAL SECRETE AN OILY SUBSTANCE TO KEEP THE FUR FROM GETTING WATERLOGGED

---

southern seals eat krill as well as squid, fish, and rockhopper penguins. Since the demise of the great baleen whales, the krill population has expanded and the seal populations are booming.

The Cape fur seal is found on the southern coasts of Africa around the Cape of Good Hope, while a very similar subspecies is resident along the coasts of New South Wales (Australia) and Tasmania. Largest of all the fur seals, the adult males are nearly

8 ft (2.4 m) long and weigh about 770 lbs (350 kg). The females are only about one-third that size. Although they both feed on fish, squid, octopus, and rock lobsters, Cape fur seals rarely dive deeper than 150 ft (45 m) while Australian fur seals feed at more than 400 ft (120 m).

Discovered in 1773 on Captain Cook's second voyage, the New Zealand fur seals were nearly wiped out by seal hunters. A species with no predators except for humans, they have been protected since 1875; the population has slowly recovered and is now about 40,000 strong.

The breeding places of the northern fur seal were also being eagerly sought by 18th-century explorers. The Russians found the first breeding beaches in the Commander Islands along the Kamchatka peninsula, but from the pattern of seal migration it was clear that larger breeding grounds must exist somewhere in the east Bering Sea. Gavril Pribylov finally discovered the islands, named Pribilof in his honor, in 1786.

At that time there were between two and four million northern fur seals, as well as numerous sea otters and walrus, in residence during the summer. A continental shelf surrounds the volcanic Pribilof

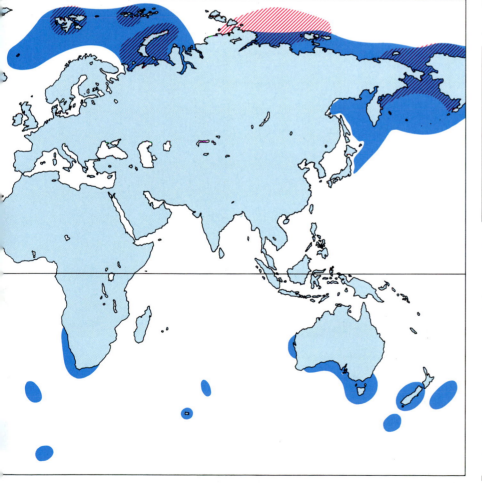

FOREST SEA LION

Rich Kirchner/NHPA

Hooker's sea lion, known also as the New Zealand or Auckland sea lion, is extremely unusual in that it is often found sheltering inland in the forests of Enderby Island, one of the Auckland Islands. Seeking the forest to escape the strong winds and driving rains means an overland journey of some 1.2 miles (2 km)—no mean feat, even for an eared seal.

As well as in the forest, the Hooker's sea lion is often seen resting on the grassy stretches of turf on top of high cliffs. In the breeding season the male puts on a ceremonial display in defense of its patch.

Islands to a depth of about 330 ft (100 m). South-westerly currents from the Pacific well up around the edge of the shelf, bearing rich schools of fish, which also support an abundant population of seabirds.

Although populations have fluctuated in response to hunting pressure, northern fur seal colonies still survive in the Pribilofs, the Commander Islands, Robben Island off Sakhalin, and in the Kuril Islands. Much farther south, a small breeding colonly was discovered on San Miguel Island off the California coast in 1968. Many of the seals found there bore identification tags, which proved they had been born in the Pribilof and Commander Islands. Generally, northern fur seals move away from their breeding grounds in search of food each winter, but the San Miguel seals remain there year-round.

Southern sea lions are found on both the Atlantic and the Pacific coasts of South America, from Uruguay around to the Peruvian seaboard. Large populations exist in the Uruguayan islands such as Isla de Lobos, and substantial breeding colonies are found in Argentina, the Falkland Islands, and Tierra del Fuego. Now protected in Chile, the southern sea lion population there is slowly building up again. Where the population is high, all suitable areas of the coast are occupied by sea lions during the breeding season. Oceanic killer

FOCUS ON
GALAPAGOS ISLANDS

The Galápagos Islands lie along the line of the equator off the coast of Ecuador in South America. They are home to many animals unique to the islands, including the Galápagos fur seal, the smallest of the otariids and found nowhere else in the world. The main colonies lie on the islands of Isabel and Fernandina, which are used year-round; these seals have no need to migrate. They feed at night on squid and small schooling fish, which congregate in the rich oceanic upwellings just offshore. As there is no pressure to migrate, the females are not forced to wean their pups at an early age; they suckle them for about two years.

Galápagos sea lions (a subspecies of the California sea lion) are found throughout the archipelago, but they breed on different beaches. Although they are smaller than California sea lions, they are twice the size of the Galápagos fur seals; adult males weigh around 440 lb (200 kg) and females 110–220 lb (50–100 kg). Like the fur seals, the Galápagos sea lions feed in Pacific upwellings, but there is the minimum of competition between them. The fur seals feed at night, while the Galápagos sea lions fish in daylight. This suits the sea lions, which find it hard to keep cool and prefer to be in the water during the heat of the day.

TEMPERATURE AND RAINFALL

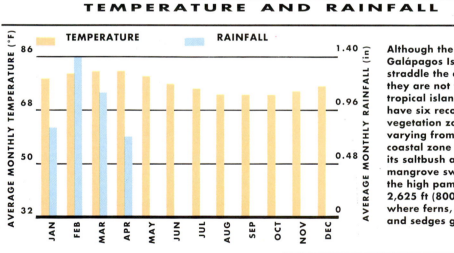

Average monthly temperature (°F) and average monthly rainfall (in) by month, January through December.

Although the Galápagos Islands straddle the equator, they are not typical tropical islands. They have six recognized vegetation zones, varying from the coastal zone with its saltbush and mangrove swamps, to the high pampa above 2,625 ft (800 m), where ferns, grasses, and sedges grow.

whales patrol the coasts of Peninsula Valdes, Argentina, where they kill large numbers of pups and sometimes adults, too. The youngsters are most vulnerable when they are about a month old and playing at the edge of the sea. The killer whales have developed a technique of charging close to the beach, rolling up the sand to seize a victim, then rolling back into the water. A persistent family of killer whales can kill up to twenty pups in the space of an hour. ∎

NEIGHBORS

Seemingly bleak in many places, the volcanic islands of the Galápagos support a unique profusion of wildlife, the most unusual of which are the giant turtles.

MARINE IGUANAS

Looking like relics from a prehistoric era, marine iguanas sunbathe before entering the water to feed.

MOCKINGBIRD

The Galápagos mockingbird has evolved to handle life on extremely arid islands.

Illustrations Kim Thompson

CONVERGING CURRENTS AROUND GALAPAGOS

The islands are renowned for the cold currents that flow north and west from the Antarctic, making the surrounding waters much colder than might be expected for an equatorial region, but also rich in nutrients.

Equator

GALAPAGOS ISLANDS

ENEMIES

EXTREMELY DANGEROUS

KILLER WHALE
Preys on sea lion pups, in particular, rolling up onto the beaches to seize a victim and dragging it into the water.

MODERATELY DANGEROUS

GREAT WHITE SHARK
Less of a threat than the killer whale, it will, nevertheless, take seals and sea lions in the water.

GREAT FRIGATE BIRD

Males of this oceangoing species are distinguished by the large, scarlet throat pouch.

GALAPAGOS TORTOISE

Harvested in thousands for meat on ships, the giant tortoises are the "galápagos" for which the islands are named.

LAVA LIZARD

These reptiles inhabit the old lava flows of these volcanic islands.

CORMORANT

The only flightless cormorant in the world, it survives in an area rich in bird life.

GALAPAGOS PENGUIN

This is the only place in the world where penguins and fur seals occur together, owing to the cold currents.

FOOD AND FASTING

GRABBING TEETH
*Needing their front
flippers to propel them
through the water, prey
is grabbed by the
mouth. The teeth possess
sharp cusps, which are
adapted for grabbing
and holding prey.*

Although fishermen blame seals for taking large quantities of fish, in fact the bulk of the diet of most seals is composed of noncommercial species such as lampreys, octopus, crustaceans, and squid. Lampreys are parasitic on salmon, so it is thought that seal activity—far from depleting the salmon population—may actually enhance it. Antarctic fur seals depend on krill, and much of the prey of other species is very small. An analysis of food eaten by California sea lions at San Miguel Island showed that they caught 90 percent squid, together with some Pacific whiting and juvenile rockfish. The average weight of the fish was 1.6 oz (45 g).

Steller sea lions take not only fish but young ringed seals and sea otters when they get the opportunity. They patrol northern fur seal breeding grounds, attacking the pups just as they are entering the water for the first time to learn to swim. Steller sea lions are thought to kill up to 6 percent of the pups born on the Pribilofs.

Although habits vary with the species, most eared seals fish at night, with two peaks of activity: just after dusk and shortly before dawn. Plankton rises toward the surface at night in what is known as the deep scattering layer, and it is here that fish—and seals—come to feed. Only sea lions capable of diving to considerable depths can reach the deep scattering layer during the day.

in SIGHT

FASTING

Female seals usually fast for a few days when they come ashore to give birth, but sexually active males go without food for up to three months. They put on as much weight as possible before the breeding season, but once the females arrive—such is the competition for a mate—they dare not take time off to feed. Although fasting seals may feel hungry, they do not starve because they are able to use the lipids stored in their blubber to keep metabolism normal. After the breeding season, both sexes fast while they are molting.

Main illustration Chris Turnbull/Wildlife Art Agency

T. S. McCann/Oxford Scientific Films

PENGUINS

These birds are sometimes taken by the subantarctic fur seal. Fur seals also feed on fish, crustaceans, and cephalopods.

ADAPTATIONS

When diving, the seal's nostrils close. It has a special closing device at the back of the throat to prevent it from taking in water when grabbing prey.

DIVES

Most fur seal dives do not last longer than five minutes. However, the Cape fur seal can make dives of below 330 ft (100 m) deep.

AMAZING FACTS

EATING ROCKS

Many species of seals have been known to eat stones. Loads of up to 20 lbs (9 kg) of pebbles, sand, and even sharp rocks have been found in the stomachs of southern sea lions. Nobody has ever really figured out why. Perhaps the stones help grind up the food or help control parasites. It may be that the stones are useful for ballast. Or perhaps they allay the pangs of hunger when a seal is fasting.

When seals dive a reflex closes their nostrils and they stop breathing, conserving oxygen by slowing the blood circulation around the body, sending it to only the essential organs. The heartbeat slows to one-tenth of its rate at the surface. When bubbles of dissolved nitrogen get into the bloodstream of human divers, they suffer crippling pain called the bends. Seals avoid this condition because the lungs of marine mammals are designed to collapse under pressure. Residual air is forced back into the windpipe, so that nitrogen cannot be absorbed into the bloodstream.

Seals hear in air as well as humans do, but they have much better directional hearing underwater. This enables them to find food in poor visibility and

PREY

OCTOPUS

LAMPREY

SWIMMING CRAB

PENGUIN

CRAYFISH

Prey illustrations Sandra Pond/Wildlife Art Agency

to keep in touch with one another. Their eyes are large and well adapted to dim light underwater, but seals do not depend on their eyesight to catch fish. Blind seals have no difficulty in feeding, and tests with California sea lions have proven that they can find food quicker in total darkness than in daylight. Although the seal has no highly developed temporal lobes in the brain to analyze sound, it is thought that they emit clicks, pulses, whistles, and warbles underwater and use the

---

ALTHOUGH A SEAL'S EYESIGHT IS EXCELLENT UNDERWATER, IT DOES NOT DEPEND ON EYESIGHT TO LOCATE PREY

---

echo to navigate or to catch prey. The seal's ears pick up the sonar resonances, but its whiskers also act as antennae, for they are sensitive to the underwater vibrations of even the tiniest fish or crustacean at close range and help the seal direct its mouth toward the food.

Deep-diving is an exhausting business, and seals always rest longer on the surface of the water in between dives if the fish are lying deep. South

AMAZING FACTS

Anthony Bannister/NHPA

The Cape fur seal is found on the most southerly tip of South Africa around the Cape of Good Hope. It is the largest of the fur seals, at about 8 ft (2.4 m). During the breeding season in December, the females give birth to their pups. They remain on the beach with their pups for about a week, then leave them to go feed. During the time the mothers are away, the seal pups are preyed upon by black-backed jackals and hyenas. This natural predation and humans who hunt by license account for the loss of up to 60 percent of all pups.

ARRIVAL ON SHORE
Many male eared seals build up as much fat as they can before they arrive at the breeding sites. This is usually a few days or weeks before the females arrive.

HEAD SHAKING
Having selected a suitable site, the seals defend it from other males using head-shaking postures and barking.

LUNGES
All fighting between males is done with the teeth and by pushing with the torso. Once a territory has been established, the dominant male awaits the arrival of his harem.

KEY FACTS

● The word *Pinnipedia,* which scientifically describes seals, is derived from two Latin words. *Pinna* means a wing feather and *pes* (genitive, *pedis*) means foot.

● Until this century fur seals were called sea bears or sea wolves.

● The longest seal whiskers on record were found on an Antarctic fur seal bull. They measured nearly 19 in (48 cm) long.

● Bull northern fur seals spend two months without food or much sleep, wearing themselves out with fighting and mating. It nearly kills them. While females normally breed for ten years or more and often live to the age of twenty-five, males seldom breed for more than one-and-a-half seasons. No males older than seventeen years have ever been found.

● Most seals give birth to their pups at the same time each year. This reduces the effect of predation by gulls, foxes, killer whales, and sharks on the population.

● More than 400,000 tourists a year visit Puerto Madryn in Chubut, Argentina, to see South American fur seals and southern sea lions. That's more tourists than sea lions!

African fur seals make dives averaging only two minutes, although they can stay underwater for up to seven minutes at a time. Sea lions dive deeper than fur seals—perhaps because they are more powerful swimmers. Galápagos fur seals seldom dive deeper than 65 ft (20 m), but Galápagos sea lions normally fish at twice that depth and have been recorded at depths of 612 ft (187 m).

Fur seals feed mainly at night and may dive to depths of 600 ft (183 m) in search of small schooling fish and squid. They eat over sixty species of prey, depending on what is available. Near the Pribilof Islands they depend on pollack, herring, capelin, and squid. ■

Illustration Steve Kingston

LIFE CYCLE

Although sea mammals such as whales and manatees pass their entire lives in water, having severed all links with the land, seals give birth and suckle their pups on land, and often mate onshore as well. The choice of a breeding site is a very important one, on which the future of many thousands (perhaps millions) of animals depends. For this reason, it is not left to chance. Both males and females are genetically programmed to return to the place of their birth to breed.

Eared seals have an annual cycle that begins just before the start of the breeding season, when males come ashore to establish their territories. A few weeks later, shortly before they are ready to give birth, the females come ashore. Studies of marked northern fur seals have shown that they try to return to the exact site of their own birth—to within a few feet. Mothers-to-be jostle with their sisters and maybe their own mothers for the same area on the beach.

Five times larger than females, male northern fur seals (*Callorhinus ursinus*) might easily be mistaken for a separate species. During the breeding season the males are an unpleasant sight. Bloodshot eyes rolling, neck dripping with blood from half a dozen wounds, in a state of crazed aggression, they attempt to control the beach. The stakes are high. Only the strongest get to breed and pass on their genes.

The most successful males are those that manage to establish a territory in the center of the breeding beach, where the natural concentration of females is thickest. If a bull can lay claim to a few square yards here, his worries are partly over. The females will come to him. However, he will be surrounded on all sides by belligerent rival males, some with established territories of their own and others intent on engaging him in battle in order to drive him off his patch. To survive the breeding season, a male must be in his prime. Few males are powerful enough to command a territory before they are nine years old, and among northern fur seals, males last an average of one-and-a-half seasons. Older "has-beens" and juvenile males are relegated to traditional hauling grounds (where there are no females) nearby.

Birth is not a complicated procedure, for the pup is a convenient torpedo shape and slithers into the world, head or tail first, quite easily. It starts

AMAZING FACTS

DELAYED IMPLANTATION

After mating, the fertilized egg develops into a hollow ball of cells called a blastocyst. This lies dormant in the seal's womb for about four months until the most crucial stage of feeding the previous pup is over. Then the blastocyst implants itself into the wall of the womb and begins to develop normally. Delayed implantation allows seals to give birth on land, then mate immediately afterward. Unlike other seals, Australian sea lions give birth every eighteen months, which suggests a longer pregnancy.

BEACH MASTERS

Only the strongest males earn the name of beach master. They are the ones to establish a "harem" and are able to breed.

WEANING

The length of time pups take to be weaned depends on the species. The time varies from four months to a year.

SUCKLING

In many species the female suckles the young for about a week, then goes to sea to feed herself. She returns at intervals of five or six days. Other species feed the pups much more often.

GROWING UP

The life of a young seal

FROM BIRTH TO DEATH

NORTHERN FUR SEAL

GESTATION: 51 WEEKS
LITTER SIZE: USUALLY 1
WEIGHT AT BIRTH: 10–12 LB
(4.5–5.4 KG)
WEANING: 3–4 MONTHS

SEXUAL MATURITY: MALES 5–6
YEARS; FEMALES 3–7 YEARS
LONGEVITY IN THE WILD: UP TO
30 YEARS

CALIFORNIA SEA LION

GESTATION: 50 WEEKS
LITTER SIZE: USUALLY 1
WEIGHT AT BIRTH: 13.5 LB
(6 KG)
WEANING: 1 YEAR

SEXUAL MATURITY: MALES 9
YEARS; FEMALES 6–8 YEARS
LONGEVITY IN THE WILD: NOT
KNOWN (30 IN CAPTIVITY)

WALRUS

GESTATION: 15–16 MONTHS
WEIGHT AT BIRTH: 140 LB
(63 KG)

WEANING: 2 YEARS
LONGEVITY IN THE WILD: 40
YEARS

MATING

*Immediately after each
female has given birth,
the beach master will
mate with her.*

Simon Turvey/Wildlife Art Agency

suckling within a few hours, and initially the mother seal stays by its side.

The Antarctic fur seal and the northern fur seal
pups get barely a week's attention before their
mothers leave to go fishing. They return once every
five or six days to suckle their offspring with a highly concentrated form of milk. The pups put on
weight rapidly and are ready to be weaned by four
months old. As soon as the pups reach 40 percent
of their adult size, the mothers lose interest and the
pups are abandoned to catch their own food.

Sea lions and fur seals, which give birth in
warmer waters, suckle their offspring for much
longer. There's plenty of food just offshore so their
absences from the breeding beach are short. The
mothers have a stronger bond with their pups and
appear to be more caring.   ■

WALRUS

TUSK LENGTH

Tusks can reach 3.3 ft (1 m) long in an adult male walrus.

No animal more symbolizes the Arctic wastes and freezing oceans than the huge, seemingly cumbersome walrus. Found in the coastal regions of the Arctic Ocean and adjoining seas, walruses were once the most abundant pinnipeds in the Pacific Ocean.

Most closely related to the eared seals, the walrus is nevertheless a larger, considerably lumpier animal. Its body is covered with short, thick hairs that get progressively more sparse as the animal gets older. In addition, the males shed most of their hair in an annual molt, at which time they appear almost naked, revealing raised protuberances on the neck and shoulders. Their skin is 0.8–1.6 in (2–4 cm) thick, with an underlying layer of blubber.

The walrus has a comparatively small, rounded head with tiny eyes and scarcely visible ears. Its large muzzle is dotted with masses of highly sensitive whiskers. The most noticeable feature of all is the long tusks that grow down from the upper jaw and are present in adults of both sexes.

Like eared seals and sea lions, the walrus can turn its hind limbs forward for use with the forelimbs when walking on land. Unlike these other animals, however, the walrus uses its hind limbs to propel itself through the water with its forelimbs acting as rudders.

The walrus spends a prodigious amount of its time in the water. It hauls out onto rocky shores or drifting pack ice to rest, to molt, and to give birth. It is mainly during this haul-out activity that its tusks

TUSKS FOR FIGHTING

Males, in particular, use their tusks to fight each other for prime positions. Deep, penetrating wounds can be inflicted with them.

HAULING OUT

The principal use of the the walrus's tusks is to help in heaving its enormous body out of the water onto the ice or rocks.

BREATHING HOLES

Tusks are also used for cutting through ice to open breathing holes or for hooking over the ice to give stability while resting or sleeping in the water.

are useful. By and large, the walrus is a migratory animal, moving south with the Arctic ice in the winter and returning north as the ice recedes in the summer.

Bivalve mollusks—clams, cockles, and mussels—are the principal food of these enormous animals, although they do eat numbers of other marine invertebrates. They find their food by diving to the ocean bottom and searching along it using their whiskers, which are extremely sensitive to touch. Items located in the mud are either dislodged by rooting with the snout or by squirting a jet of water into the preys' holes. The animal is removed from its shell by powerful suction,

WHISKERS

Whiskers are used to find food on the seabed.

in SIGHT

A male walrus indulges in an elaborate and noisy courtship display to attract a female from her resting position on land. In a water "dance," he puts his head beneath the water and emits a series of clicks and bell-like sounds. He then lifts his head and makes further sharp clicks and whistles. Noises are made through a pair of pouches in the cheeks, which resonate and amplify sound.

and the shells are discarded. It is thought that a walrus eats thousands of mollusks at a feeding session. It can stay underwater for up to ten minutes and generally forages at depths of 80–100 ft (24–30 m).

Although walrus are gregarious—males and females will huddle together in huge single-sex groups on rocks or ice floes—older males bully younger ones for prime positions. During the mating season in January and February, males fight for prime positions in the water, just off land, where numbers of females congregate. Mating takes place in the water.

As with seals and sea lions, implantation of the fetus is delayed, so the total gestation lasts some 15–16 months. Only one young is born, fully developed and able to swim. It forms a stronger bond with the mother than any other pinniped does, and it also seems likely that females will take care of other pups that have been abandoned for any reason. The young usually continue suckling for two years, although they will have begun to forage for food by then.

Pups do not reach sexual maturity until the age of eight to ten years for males and six to seven years for females. ∎

SLAUGHTER AND RECOVERY

SEALS HAVE BEEN SACRIFICED TO THE FASHION TRADE EVER SINCE THE INTERNATIONAL MARKET FOR FURS BOOMED TWO CENTURIES AGO. TODAY THERE ARE OTHER EXCUSES FOR KILLING THEM

We know from Stone Age engravings that humans have been killing seals for thousands of years. The blubber that keeps seals warm was also used to protect humans from the cold, either rendered into fuel oil or eaten raw. Warm sealskin clothing made life possible for hunters along the coasts of the North Pacific and the North Atlantic. At the tip of South America, on Tierra del Fuego, the Indians depended so heavily on seals that when European hunters exterminated them, the Indians starved.

Small-scale subsistence hunting had little impact on seal populations, but in the 17th and 18th centuries an international market for furs developed. Fur seals were particularly sought after because of the quality of their thick coats. During the 19th century, Chinese furriers developed a method of removing the coarse guard hairs from the pelt to expose the soft underfur. As a result, millions of seals were slaughtered to make garments, and the fur trade became more lucrative.

When Russia sold Alaska to the United States in 1867, the Americans were able to recoup the entire purchase price of $7,200,000 from the sale of northern fur seal pelts (from the Pribilof Islands) within the space of six years. In other parts of the world, large fur seal colonies such as those in the South Shetland Islands were decimated by get-rich-quick sailors almost as soon as they were discovered. The greed of the sealers was insatiable. They killed every seal they could lay their hands on—not only pups, but adult females of breeding age as well. As populations crashed, sealers began chasing seals on the open sea.

No species of eared seal actually became extinct, but the Juan Fernandez, Galápagos, and Guadalupe fur seals came perilously close to destruction. The Galápagos fur seals were so heavily hunted that the species was believed to be extinct in 1900, but a few survived the slaughter and the population has slowly built to around 40,000.

FATE OF NORTHERN FUR SEALS

Although they were not discovered until the late 18th century, the northern fur seals of the Pribilof Islands were soon in danger. Forty thousand were killed in the first year of exploitation alone, and perhaps two-and-a-half million died between 1786 and 1867. Finally reason prevailed. Rather than kill the goose that laid the golden egg by driving the seals to extinction, it was decided to manage the valuable

Workers place a dead seal covered in oil into a plastic bag (right). *The spill from the tanker Braer has claimed the lives of hundreds .*

S. Krasemann/NHPA

L. Cironneau/Associated Press/Topham

Large-scale culling of northern fur seals, St. Paul Island, Pribilof (Alaska), has now largely ceased.

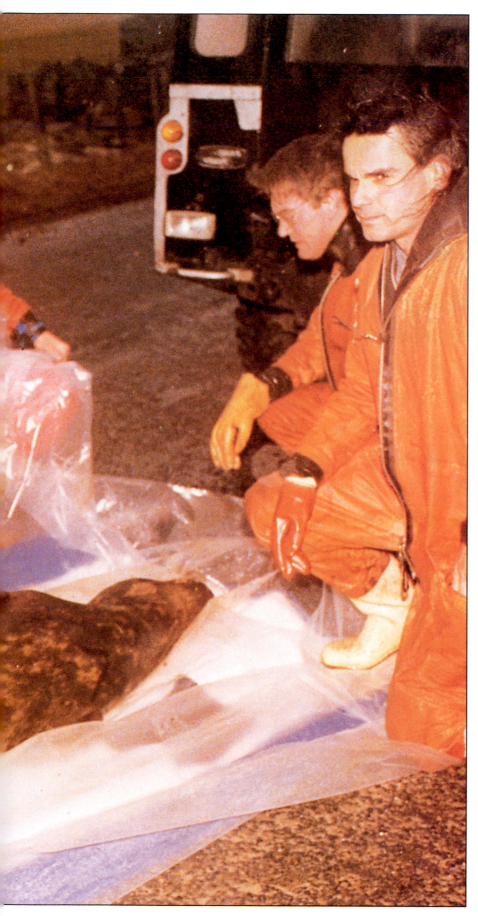

THEN & NOW

This chart shows the amount of fish taken by the Steller sea lion (top) and the walrus (bottom).

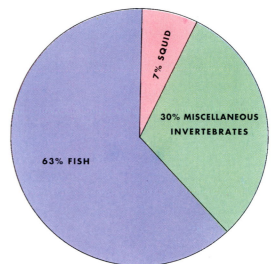

7% SQUID

30% MISCELLANEOUS INVERTEBRATES

63% FISH

Steller sea lions have a diet that consists of over 50 percent fish, which is why it is hated by Canadian salmon fishermen. However, the amount of salmon eaten by both sea lions and harbor seals in British Columbia amounts to only 2.5 percent of the commercial catch. Sea lions observed feeding at the mouth of the Rogue River in Oregon ate 87 percent lampreys and only 2 percent salmon. (The other 11 percent was not identifiable.) Since lamprey eels are parasitic on salmon, the activities of sea lions probably increase the salmon population.

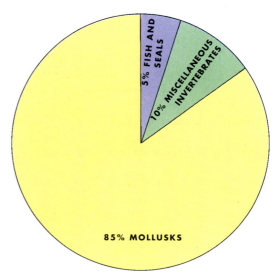

5% FISH AND SEALS

10% MISCELLANEOUS INVERTEBRATES

85% MOLLUSKS

herds in the interests of all the sealing nations.

In an attempt to stabilize the population and to achieve maximum "productivity," the governments of Japan, Great Britain (for Canada), Imperial Russia, and the United States met in 1911 to form the North Pacific Fur Seal Commission. Pelagic sealing was prohibited, and it was agreed that the Russians should retain control of the Commander Island, Robben Island, and Kuril herds, while the United States would control the Pribilof seals. Canada and Japan were to receive a percentage of the skins in return for abstaining from sealing. Although it was a strictly commercial treaty—designed to make money not to protect seals—the agreement allowed the fur seal herds to recover. Only young male seals between the ages of two and five years were to be killed. Nevertheless, harvests during the period 1980–1984 produced between 22,000 and 26,000 pelts. Sealing continued on the Pribilof Islands until 1985, but it has now largely ceased. Today, only a small number of seals, which are needed for subsistence by the Aleut population, are killed.

During the period that fur seals were harvested, their biology was carefully researched in order to protect them as a valuable commercial resource. Over the years this attitude has mellowed. Today

Topham

SEALS IN DANGER

BECAUSE OF THE 1972 ENDANGERED SPECIES ACT SEALS OFF THE COAST OF THE UNITED STATES ARE PROTECTED FROM HUNTING, AND MOST POPULATIONS ARE INCREASING. IT IS AN OFFENSE TO HARM OR DISTURB SEALS IN ANY WAY, AND EVEN SCIENTISTS MUST HAVE A SPECIAL PERMIT TO STUDY THEM. ONLY TWO SPECIES OF EARED SEALS ARE VULNERABLE:

GUADALUPE FUR SEAL	VULNERABLE ESTIMATED POPULATION: 500–2,500
JUAN FERNANDEZ FUR SEAL	VULNERABLE ESTIMATED POPULATION: 6,000–8,000

***VULNERABLE* MEANS THAT THE SPECIES IS LIKELY TO BECOME ENDANGERED IN THE NEAR FUTURE UNLESS STEPS ARE TAKEN TO PROTECT IT.**

ALONGSIDE MAN

TOURISM AND SEALS

The plight of seals and other marine mammals has touched the hearts of many people. However, this new public awareness brings its own problems. Tourism to far-off places is increasing to such an extent that this in itself causes problems for the animals the tourist are seeking to see.

Many seals are shy in their own environments. Others, like the California sea lion, are exceeding playful at all times. However, even some California sea lions, like the one above, do not take kindly to tourists getting too close when they have hauled out onto the beaches to rest or give birth. This incident happened in Santa Fe on the Galápagos Islands, a nature preserve where both plants and animals are strictly protected. Situations like this are monitored carefully, for countries cannot afford to lose the revenue that the tourists bring with them.

Richard Coomber/Planet Earth Pictures

fur seal and sea lion populations are monitored and protected for quite different reasons. There has been a complete change in attitude toward seals.

Australian fur seals are fully protected, but in South Africa, Cape fur seals are still hunted both summer and winter. Quotas are established and licenses issued under the (misleadingly named) Sea Birds and Seal Protection Act of 1973. In Uruguay fishermen kill large numbers of southern sea lions, and there is also a government cull, the argument

OVER ONE MILLION NORTHERN FUR SEALS WERE KILLED BY SEALERS FROM 1868 TO 1911

being that fish stocks need to be protected.

Although most populations of seals in the world are increasing, numbers of Steller sea lions in the east Bering Sea are dwindling alarmingly. Seabird populations in that area have crashed, and no one can account for a mysterious failure of the northern fur seals to thrive. Many explanations have been discussed. Pollution such as the *Exxon Valdez* oil spill in Prince William Sound, Alaska, could be contributing to the environmental decline. Perhaps global warming or changes in the pattern of ocean currents are to blame. Coincidentally, the Alaskan walleye pollack fishery is now the biggest in the world. ∎

INTO THE FUTURE

Although seals are familiar animals to us, their habitat—the ocean—remains largely a mystery. We still know very little about how seals interact with their environment. Scientists are now studying fur seals closely in an attempt to share their knowledge. Time-and-depth recorders are strapped on to seals to record their fishing habits. Scientists think that seals navigate by "tasting" the salinity of the ocean as they follow currents to find the rich upwellings where fish congregate. The ocean covers two-thirds of the surface of our planet, and changes taking place within it are of crucial significance, not only for the survival of seals but for our own future.

With culling restricted in many areas, it would appear that the safety of seals has been ensured. Unfortunately, this is not so. Another perhaps greater danger threatens. The overfishing of the oceans leaves little for the seals, and the techniques

PREDICTION

BIODEGRADABLE NETS

To save seals and other marine mammals from unnecessary suffering from discarded nets, conservation organizations are calling for the introduction of biodegradable nets.

used for catching what seafood there is results in many seals dying in the long drift nets of fishermen.

The story is the same all around the world. Overfishing by high-tech fishing boats has caused populations of important commercial fish such as cod, herring, and salmon to crash. Governments have been slow to confront their own fishing industries, and controls have been imposed on international fishing fleets too late.

The North Sea's European fishery is exhausted. The vast shoals that were once found to the Grand Banks of Newfoundland have vanished. The enormous anchovy fishery off the Peruvian coast collapsed in the 1970s with the loss of countless millions of seabirds and mammals. The South Atlantic, which is the territory of another great international fishing fleet, also has its mysteries. The population of southern sea lions has fallen from 400,000 to barely 30,000 in the Falkland Islands. (The world population is about 240,000.) ■

PROTECTED AREAS

William M. Smithey/Planet Earth Pictures

Between 1980 and 1992, a fleet of up to 300 huge fishing vessels each set 31 mi (50 km) of drift net every night across the North Pacific to catch squid. Although it is now illegal for boats to set drift nets longer than 3 mi (5 km), this wall of death continues to drown millions of seals, whales, and seabirds every year. Even short drift nets cause casualties. Some seals sometimes manage to break free, but they are a distressing sight on the rocks, for the plastic line cuts into their flesh, causing terrible wounds and a lingering death.

FLUCTUATING NUMBERS

The northern fur seal has always borne the brunt of the sealers' clubs and nets. Their numbers have fluctuated heavily, depending on the mood of the governments concerned with culling them for one reason or another. From an original population of over two million animals, by the early 1900s the Pribilof Island herds were estimated as being between 150,000 and 300,000.

For five years, between 1912 and 1917, pelagic sealing of the Pribilof Island herds was prohibited altogether. Numbers increased to near their original level, and authorized culls began again. This was not detrimental to the seals and populations continued to thrive; the seals even returned to areas that had been depleted years before.

When the natural mortality rate of the seals began to rise, it was thought that overcrowding and subsequent disease were causing the early deaths. Again it was decided to reduce the numbers by culling. The mortality rate has not improved for the seals, and it has been thought that too many females were sacrificed and the development of the pollack fishing industry have kept numbers low.

TRUE SEALS

True seals belong to the family Phocidae in the order Pinnipedia. Members of the same order include:

WALRUS

NORTHERN FUR SEAL

SOUTHERN FUR SEAL

CALIFORNIA SEA LION

STELLER SEA LION

SOUTHERN SEA LION

E. & P. Bauer/ZEFA

True seals comprise one of three families in the order Pinnipedia; they are characterized by their hind-limb swimming technique and poor locomotion on land. The other families are the Otariidae, or eared seals, and the Odobenidae, which consists of a single species: the walrus.

ORDER

Pinnipedia
(seals and sea lions)

FAMILY

Phocidae
(true seals)

SUBFAMILIES
Monachinae
(southern seals)
Phocinae
(northern seals)

10 GENERA

19 SPECIES

Antarctic (4)
bearded (1)
elephant (2)
hooded (1)
monk (3)
white-coated (8)

S**TREAMLINED** S**WIMMERS**

A**LTHOUGH THEIR DOGLIKE HEADS BETRAY THEIR ORIGINS AS DISTANT**
R**ELATIVES OF THE LAND CARNIVORES, THE TRUE SEALS CAN RIVAL THE**
W**HALES AND FISH AS MASTERS OF THEIR AQUATIC ENVIRONMENT**

When Christopher Columbus ordered his hungry crew to butcher eight "sea wolves" for their supper while exploring the coast of Hispaniola in 1494, and while still presumably under the impression that he was among the spice islands of the East, his zoological instinct served him better than his sense of geography. For while many of his contemporaries still chose to regard seals as aberrant fish—a view that incidentally permitted

them to eat seal meat during Lent, a time to abstain from meat—Columbus correctly identified the monk seals of the Caribbean as not only mammals, but relatives of the carnivores: the order that includes the wolves, all other dogs, cats, bears, and weasels.

Discounting the walrus, which is classified in a family of its own, there are two basic types of seals: the true (or hair) seals of the family Phocidae (FOKE-id-eye) with 19 species, and the eared seals of the family Otariidae (o-tar-EYE-id-eye) with

14 species. Fossil evidence indicates that both types evolved from land-dwelling carnivores, but the eared seals—a group that includes the fur seals and sea lions—probably arose from doglike stock, while the apparently earless true seals evolved from otterlike ancestors related to the weasels. This distinction is not just academic, for although the two types have acquired a superficial resemblance owing to their shared way of life, this similarity masks profound differences in structure.

SIGNS OF TRUE SEALS

The most important of these differences concern their limbs and swimming techniques. The basic five-toed limbs of both types have evolved into flippers, but while the sea lions and their eared allies can use their flippers as functional legs, enabling them to stand on all fours and get around on land with some agility (occasionally balancing balls on their noses), the true seals have abandoned the concept of legs altogether. A true seal's forelimbs are much shorter than those of an eared seal and barely strong enough to support its weight; meanwhile, its hind limbs project to the rear instead of forward under its body, and have no function at all on land. Consequently the true seal is forced to move overland by humping along on its chest and stomach like an overgrown maggot, although some species can move at high speeds on slippery rocks and ice.

In the water the differences are equally marked. An eared seal uses its long, powerful forelimbs in

Liz & Tony Bomford/Ardea

P. Reynolds/Frank Lane Picture Agency

The bearded seal (above) *uses its long whiskers to help locate food on the seabed.*

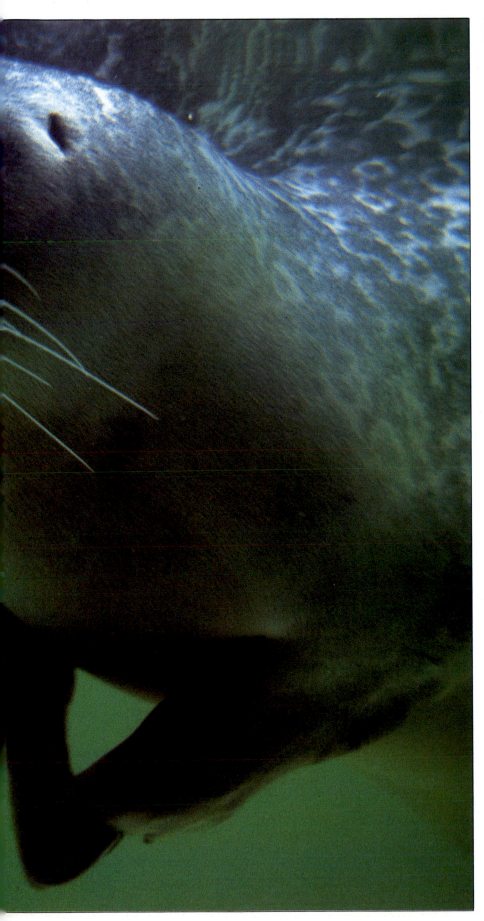

DESIGNED FOR DIVING

Deep diving involves obvious problems for air-breathing mammals, but not so for the true seal, whose special adaptations enable it to stay underwater for extended periods. A deep dive may last 30–45 minutes, and a Weddell seal once stayed underwater for an astounding 73 minutes.

Basically, seals avoid holding their breath, as big lungfuls of air would buoy them up and make diving difficult. Instead, a seal takes a deep breath, absorbs the vital oxygen into its bloodstream, empties its lungs to get rid of the carbon dioxide and nitrogen (responsible for the condition known to human divers as the bends), and then dives. To increase its oxygen storage capacity, a true seal has much more blood in its body than most mammals. Its blood is also richer in oxygen-carrying hemoglobin, and its muscles are charged with another oxygen-carrying protein called myoglobin. It can also acquire this oxygen quickly by rapidly accelerating its heart rate from roughly 40 beats per minute underwater to 120 beats per minute when it surfaces.

These arrangements enable a seal to maintain a succession of short dives indefinitely; but for really deep, long dives it has to resort to drastic measures. The heart rate drops to four or five beats per minute, and much of the blood circulation network is shut down so only the most sensitive organs are kept supplied with oxygen.

unison to row itself along or "fly" underwater like a penguin; and accordingly it has a brawny, shoulder-heavy physique, with massive neck and forelimb bones and muscles. By contrast, a true seal normally tucks its short fore flippers into its flanks and drives itself forward with alternate strokes of its hind limbs, expanding each in turn and fanning it inward and back while the other is contracted and moved forward. The flipper action is backed up by lateral undulations of the seal's very mobile hindquarters in an elegant, graceful action like that of a fish, and almost as efficient.

Indeed everything about the true seal is tailored for aquatic efficiency. The proportions of its limbs

Propelled by its powerful hind limbs, the common seal uses its forelimbs to steer through the water.

have been reduced to the bare minimum necessary for propulsion and have no supporting role whatsoever, even on land. This ensures that they create no unnecessary drag.

All other drag-inducing protrusions have been done away with: The animal has no external ear flaps (although it has fully functional ears), and the mammary glands of the female are thin sheets of tissue extending over the seal's belly and flanks; even the nipples are normally retracted to lie flush with the body surface, occasionally causing difficulty for newborn pups. The testes of the male are inside its body and cooled by chilled blood flowing back toward the heart from the hind flippers (sperm will not develop at normal body temperatures, which is why the testes of most mammals are out in the cold). Likewise, the male's penis is retracted into an internal sheath. Finally the whole body of the seal is encased in a thick layer of fatty tissue beneath the skin called blubber, smoothing the erratic contours of bone and muscle into a sleek, tapering, streamlined form that slips through the water like a torpedo. ■

THE TRUE SEALS' FAMILY TREE

Anatomically and geographically, the true seals fall into two subfamilies. The northern seals (Phocinae) have relatively weak foreflippers and powerful back muscles for propulsion; they occur in Arctic and northern cool-temperate waters. The southern seals (Monachinae) are more widespread, since they include the monk seals of Mediterranean, Caribbean, and Hawaiian waters, the northern and southern elephant seals, and four ice-breeding Antarctic species.

COMMON SEAL
Phoca vitulina (FO-ca vee-tu-LEE-na)

The common seal is one of eight species of white-coated seals that include all the seals of the genus Phoca and the gray seal. The white **infant fur of these seals is an adaptation to ice-breeding, although the gray seal may breed on land** **and the common seal has become adapted for breeding on tidal beaches in temperate waters.**

BEARDED SEAL
Erignathus barbatus (eh-rig-NATH-us bar-BAT-us)

This circumpolar species has affinities with the monk seals, including the dark lanugo (infant fur) of the newborn young, which is clearly not adapted to its ice-breeding habit. It is named for its luxuriant whiskers, which enable it to locate food on the seabed in the often cloudy, dark waters of the rich northern seas.

Ⓐ NCESTORS
ANCESTRAL WATERS
Fossil evidence indicates that the true seals originated in the northeast Atlantic some twenty-five million years ago and gradually spread north and south to colonize the icy waters of the polar regions. Anatomically, the most primitive surviving species is the Hawaiian monk seal, which seems to have reached the Pacific via the Caribbean and the Central American Seaway, the channel that separated North and South America until four or five million years ago.

HOODED SEAL
Cystophora cristata (sis-to-FOUR-ra kris-TAH-ta)

The inflatable proboscis and heavyweight build of the hooded seal are reminiscent of the elephant seals, but anatomically it has more in common with the white-coated northern seals. An ice-breeder, it occurs throughout the ice-bound regions of the North Atlantic and adjacent seas.

CRABEATER SEAL
Lobodon carcinophagus
(lob-O-don kar-sin-o-FAH-gus)

The crabeater, Weddell, leopard, and Ross seals are ice-breeding species of the far south. Denizens of the Antarctic coastal and pack ice, they exploit some of the world's richest food resources. The crabeater feeds largely on krill, the leopard seal feeds largely on penguin and crabeaters.

ELEPHANT SEALS
Mirounga (mi-ROON-ga) species

Aptly named both for the vast size of the males and for their pendulous trunklike noses, the elephant seals are notable for their polygamous breeding arrangements, in which the males fight each other for the right to mate with as many females as possible. Once heavily exploited for its blubber, which was rendered into oil, the northern elephant seal, M. angustirostris, is now thriving under strict protection. M. leonina is the southern species.

NORTHERN SEALS

SOUTHERN SEALS

SUBORDER PHOCOIDEA

MONK SEALS
Monachus (mon-AHC-us)

Of the three species of monk seals, one—the Caribbean monk seal—is almost certainly extinct as a result of exploitation and disturbance of its subtropical breeding grounds. The Hawaiian and Mediterranean monk seals are also endangered.

Color illustrations Kim Thompson

SUBORDER OTAROIDEA

SEA LIONS

FUR SEALS

WALRUS

ALL PINNIPEDS

Sea lion and walrus Robin Boutel/Fur seal Ruth Grewcock

1983

ANATOMY:
THE COMMON SEAL

The largest of the true seals is the male southern elephant seal, which regularly achieves a head-to-tail length of 16 ft (4.9 m) and a weight of 5,300 lb (2,400 kg). The smallest species is the ringed seal, which rarely grows to more than 5 ft (1.5 m) and weighs around 209 lb (95 kg).

THE BODY

is insulated against the cold by a streamlined layer of blubber. The adult coat of hair is relatively thin, since even thick fur has little insulation value in deep water.

THE EARS

have no external flaps, yet they are highly sensitive—particularly underwater, where sound travels well owing to the density of the medium. When diving, the air space in the inner ear is pressurized by a blood-filled sinus to match the increasing water pressure at greater depth.

THE EYES

are forward-facing for good binocular vision, which is essential for judging distances when hunting. They are adapted for seeing underwater, and a seal can see clearly in air only if the light is bright enough to contract its pupils to pinhole slits.

THE MUZZLE

has sharp teeth for gripping slippery fish and long sensitive whiskers for locating prey in murky water. The whiskers may be able to sense the pressure waves created by other animals, as do the lateral line sensors of fish.

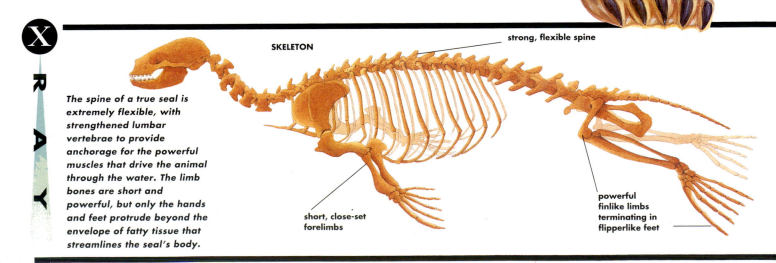

SKELETON

strong, flexible spine

The spine of a true seal is extremely flexible, with strengthened lumbar vertebrae to provide anchorage for the powerful muscles that drive the animal through the water. The limb bones are short and powerful, but only the hands and feet protrude beyond the envelope of fatty tissue that streamlines the seal's body.

short, close-set forelimbs

powerful finlike limbs terminating in flipperlike feet

X-ray illustrations Elisabeth Smith

HEAD SHAPES

From left to right: *The enlarged muzzle of the male elephant seal amplifies its roars; the powerful, thickset head of the leopard seal is adapted for preying on seals and penguins; the rounded, doglike head and big eyes of the common seal is typical of the family.*

FACT FILE:
THE COMMON SEAL

CLASSIFICATION

GENUS: *PHOCA*
SPECIES: *VITULINA*

SIZE

HEAD–BODY LENGTH: 4.9–5.6 FT (1.5–1.7 M)
WEIGHT (MALE): 240–265 LB (109–120 KG)
WEIGHT (FEMALE): 175–200 LB (79–91 KG)
WEIGHT AT BIRTH: 22–26 LB (10–12 KG)

COLORATION

ADULT: PALE TO DARK GRAY, WITH A DENSE MOTTLING OF DARKER SPOTS OR RINGS
PUP: UNUSUALLY ITS FUR IS SIMILAR TO THE ADULT, FOR THE PALE, FURRY LANUGO IS SHED IN THE WOMB

FEATURES

BROAD, ROUNDED, DOGLIKE HEAD
NO VISIBLE EARS
LARGE EYES
SLEEK, STREAMLINED BODY
SHORT FLIPPERS

THE HIND LIMBS

project backward like the tail fin of a fish and provide most of the power that drives the seal forward through the water. The feet are elongated and flattened into flippers, but the rest of each limb is shortened and contained within the body.

HIND FLIPPERS

Like all true seals of the northern subfamily, the common seal has large claws on its hind flippers, although they have little function on limbs that are primarily adapted for swimming. On southern seals, such as the southern elephant seal, the claws are greatly reduced, and the toes are strongly webbed to increase their propulsive efficiency.

THE FORELIMBS

are formed into short flippers, which are held close to the flanks during fast swimming and used for maneuvering during slow swimming. A seal may also hold large prey between its forelimbs while it tears chunks off with its teeth, like an otter.

COMMON SEAL　　**ELEPHANT SEAL**

FORELIMB AND HAND

The enlarged hand of a seal broadens the area of the limb to increase swimming performance. It also provides a degree of digital dexterity that some species find very useful when dealing with large prey.

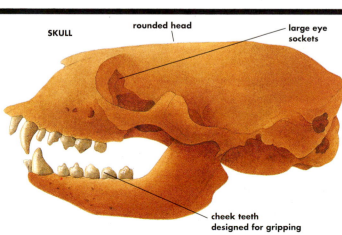

SKULL

rounded head

large eye sockets

cheek teeth designed for gripping

Unlike land carnivores, the seal's cheek teeth are not differentiated into meat-slicing carnassials and bone-cracking molars. A typical seal uses its teeth to grip rather than slice or chew, and even the strongly predatory leopard seal is poorly equipped to process its prey. The eye sockets are large to accommodate big eyes for seeing in the submarine gloom.

Illustrations Lee Gibbons/Wildlife Art Agency

MARINE MYSTERIES

ADAPTED FOR SUBMARINE EFFICIENCY, THE TRUE SEALS ARE AWKWARD AND VULNERABLE ON LAND. WHEN FORCED TO HAUL OUT OF THE WATER TO BREED OR MOLT, MOST SPECIES GET THE JOB DONE IN RECORD TIME

Doug Allan/Oxford Scientific Films

In early March, the Gulf of St. Lawrence in western Quebec, Canada, is a glittering tumult of crushed and tumbled pack ice and broad, snow-covered floes—drifting fragments of the sea ice that seals the surface of the gulf throughout the winter. Yet here and there between the floes there is a ripple of dark movement, where the spring sun and the slow drift of the pack have torn holes in the frozen crust, allowing a glimpse of the living, glass-clear water below; and through these holes emerge the whiskered heads of harp seals.

SPEEDY BIRTHS

The seals breed on the pack ice. As the grip of winter relaxes, the females swim up through the long leads of open water and haul out onto the floes, which are still at this point locked together in a great crumpled sheet. Assembling in huge aggregations of tens of thousands, yet each defending her own space, the harp seals rapidly give birth to their white-coated pups and nurse them intensively for two weeks or so, then slip back into the water to mate and disperse. As the ice starts to break up, the weaned pups follow, plunging into the chill, rich waters to begin their adult lives as creatures of the sea.

The adult seals are ashore for perhaps twenty days, while the pups linger for another two weeks. During this time they are at constant risk from predators such as polar bears, although the instability of the pack ice provides some security from land carnivores. Other species, such as the gray seal, may breed on remote islands and inaccessible beaches, while the common or harbor seal emerges at low tide, gives birth on the tidal strand, and slips back into the water as the tide floods back in, accompanied by her pup, which can swim within a few hours of birth.

For all true seals the breeding period is potentially a time of hunger and vulnerability, and although no other species has adopted the same drastic solution as the common seal, most have managed to cut their forced stay on land to a bare minimum.

ANNUAL MOLT

There is one other time when true seals are forced to come ashore. Each year a seal must shed its outer layer of skin and renew its coat of hair, and the process of molting and regrowth demands an increase in the blood supply to the skin. This enables more heat to be lost to the cold water, forcing the seal to haul out onto the beach or sea ice. In polar species this occurs in spring and summer, when the seals can bask in the 24-hour sunshine; elsewhere, elephant seals gather in tight groups, heaped one upon the other to conserve heat. The molt is soon over, though, and for the rest of the

ZEFA

The hooded seal's "red balloon" is one of two nasal displays. The other produces an inflated black "hood."

Baikal seals congregate on the shores of the landlocked Lake Baikal in Siberia.

year the seals spend most of their time at sea, hauling out to relax in the sun when it suits them, but essentially living the life they are adapted for: that of swimming, diving marine mammals.

MYSTERIOUS MAMMALS
The lives of true seals during these months at sea are still something of a mystery. The obvious difficulty of observing animals that spend much of their lives underwater is compounded by the inaccessibility and hostility of the icebound habitats of many species, and although researchers have learned a lot about seal movements by using radio tracking and similar techniques, many aspects of seal behavior have had to be deduced from scant evidence.

The subtleties of social interaction, for example, are virtually impossible to study underwater, and most of the published data is drawn from observations made during the breeding and molting periods. Their behavior at these times indicates that although many species are highly gregarious, often associating in huge herds or rookeries, their social arrangements are relatively basic. ■

KEY FACTS

● **Despite its ungainliness out of the water, the crabeater seal can achieve speeds of up to 15.5 mph (25 km/h) as it slides over the ice.**

● **Polar seals such as the ringed seal and Ross seal feed in total darkness throughout the winter months, indicating that they have highly developed tactile senses and systems of echolocation.**

● **The crabeater seal is probably the world's most numerous large mammal.**

● **The Mediterranean monk seal is one of the twelve most endangered mammals in the world.**

● **Weddell seals, which maintain airholes by biting through the sea ice, suffer badly from broken teeth and dental abcesses.**

● **A bull southern elephant seal may grow to a length of 20 ft (6 m) and weigh up to 8,800 lb (4,000 kg).**

HABITATS

The true seals are commonly associated with the freezing conditions of the Arctic and Antarctic, yet several species thrive in warm waters far from the floating pack ice of the polar seas. The common seal is found as far south as Baja California in Mexico, and the Hawaiian monk seal breeds on the subtropical shores of the Leeward Islands near Hawaii, basking on beaches of coral sand and chasing colorful fish through coral reef lagoons. A similar species of monk seal was once widespread throughout the Mediterranean, and scattered populations still survive in the few areas that have escaped development for tourism. These monk seals probably developed from stock that evolved in warm waters, and therefore have no cold-water ancestors, yet they are similar in all major respects to species that regularly endure months of subzero temperatures. The layer of blubber beneath the skin of the Hawaiian monk seal is roughly the same thickness as that of many ice-breeding species, indicating that the true seals were already well equipped to survive low temperatures long before they colonized the coldest seas on earth.

DISTRIBUTION

The true seals are widespread throughout the world, but most species are associated with the icebound seas of the polar regions. These include the ringed, harp, and hooded seals in the Arctic and the Weddell, Ross, leopard, and crabeater seals in the Antarctic. Others prefer slightly warmer waters: The southern elephant seal breeds mainly on subantarctic islands such as South Georgia, while the biggest breeding populations of gray seals occur around the northern coasts of Great Britain.

KEY

TRUE SEALS

FOCUS ON ANTARCTIC CRABEATERS

The crabeater seal is the most widespread and numerous of the Antarctic seals—indeed, with a total population of up to 40 million, it is probably the most abundant large mammal in the world. Crabeaters feed on shrimplike crustaceans, called krill, hunting by night when the krill rise from the ocean depths to feed on the plankton near the surface. By day the seals generally haul out onto the ice, where they are safe from predatory leopard seals and killer whales. Groups of crabeaters frequently bask on drifting rafts of ice, often in company with other seals and penguins, for the floes make convenient, secure floating bases with ready access to deep water. In this way a crabeater seal may spend its whole life at sea and never set a flipper on solid ground.

Jonathan Scott/Planet Earth Pictures

The excellent insulation of a true seal—any true seal—is in fact an adaptation for living in the water. Even in the tropics, ocean water is considerably colder than a seal's core temperature of 98.6°F (37°C), and the heat-conducting properties of water are so good that the animal would suffer an unacceptable loss of heat and energy if it lacked the necessary insulation. Having acquired it, however, the seals were ideally equipped to radiate north and south into colder seas and exploit some of the richest of all marine habitats.

Rich resources are the lure that draws all kinds of animals to the apparently inhospitable waters of the Arctic and Antarctic. By comparison with the land at high latitudes, the salt seawater is a sheltered environment: Until it actually freezes, the sea is far warmer than the land in winter, and there is always water under the sea ice offering a safe haven for all kinds of organisms. The polar oceans are also particularly rich in minerals scoured up from the bottom by wind-driven ocean currents, and because of their low temperature they hold a lot of dissolved carbon dioxide and oxygen. As a

IN ANTARCTICA THE WEDDELL SEAL OVERWINTERS UNDER THE ICE SHEET, SINCE THE INSULATING BLANKET OF ICE KEEPS THE SEA RELATIVELY WARM

result they are immensely fertile, providing ideal growing conditions for the floating microscopic algae called phytoplankton. These algae attract a host of tiny floating animals such as copepods and the great swarms of krill that flourish in the southern ocean; the whole teeming mass provides a feast for crustaceans, squid, and fish. These in turn attract larger animals such as seabirds, whales, and, of course, seals.

There are drawbacks, though, even for animals that do not apparently feel the cold. In winter, large areas of the sea freeze over, sometimes forcing seals to migrate to places where they still have access to the water and prey. The harp seal, for example, migrates south from its High Arctic feeding grounds to areas of broken, drifting pack ice. There are three distinct populations overwintering respectively in the warmer waters around Newfoundland, the Greenland Sea north of Jan Mayen Island, and the White Sea in northwestern Russia. The seals breed in their winter refuges and disperse to the richer waters in the north as the northern sea ice breaks up; the Newfoundland population migrates some 2,170 miles (3,500 km) to spend the summer in Baffin Bay to the west of Greenland. The larger hooded seal undertakes similar migrations, although it does not travel as far. ∎

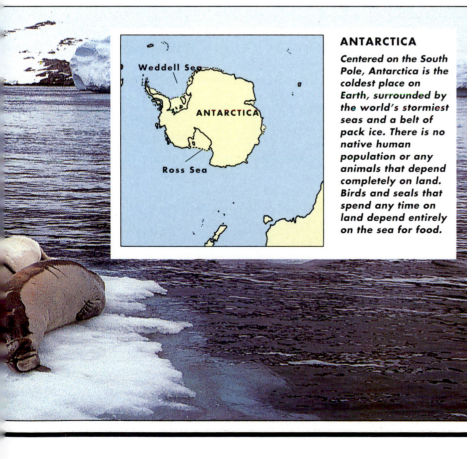

ANTARCTICA

Centered on the South Pole, Antarctica is the coldest place on Earth, surrounded by the world's stormiest seas and a belt of pack ice. There is no native human population or any animals that depend completely on land. Birds and seals that spend any time on land depend entirely on the sea for food.

HUNTING

Most true seals feed on relatively small fish and similar creatures that can be captured without too much trouble, snapped up, and swallowed whole. Their teeth reflect this: Typical seals have several more-or-less identical cheek teeth in each jaw instead of the specialized grinders and slicers that equip land carnivores for crushing bones and shearing through flesh and sinew. Most of the seal's teeth are fashioned into spikes like the jaws of a steel trap, since its main preoccupation is simply keeping a grip on its slippery, writhing prey.

DIVING FOR DINNER

The Weddell seal of the far south is typical of this fish-trap feeding style. It feeds beneath the fast ice—immobile sea ice that is still attached to the land in a continuous sheet, unlike the drifting, fragmented pack ice—and makes forays from a

---

IF A WEDDELL SEAL CATCHES A REALLY BIG FISH, IT WILL RETURN TO THE SURFACE TO TEAR IT TO PIECES

---

breathing hole that it cuts through the ice with its teeth. It feeds mainly on fish, taking active midwater species, such as the Antarctic cod, as well as crustaceans and squid, which it chases through the water with sharklike speed and agility. When it catches up with a potential victim, it lunges forward to grab it in its jaws, juggles it rapidly, and swallows it headfirst to prevent any spiny fin rays from lodging in its throat.

Hunting mainly by sight in the blue gloom beneath the ice, the Weddell seal typically dives for 8 to 15 minutes at a time, surfacing for brief respites of 2 to 4 minutes between dives. Its breathing hole is normally sited at a point of natural weakness with several radiating cracks, and these cracks may help the seal locate the hole as it surfaces for air. The first few dives from a newly cut hole are rather tentative as the seal gets its bearings, but as it gains confidence it swims farther and deeper, and may dive to the seabed for slow, bottom-living fish. These dives are much deeper and more prolonged, often reaching depths of 980–1,300 ft (300–400 m), but a Weddell seal has been recorded diving to 1,970 ft (600 m) in a round-trip lasting over an hour. Such long dives are unusual, however, and are rarely attempted when darkness makes visual navigation difficult; at

such times, Weddell seals probably avoid excursions into unfamiliar territory and stay close to their breathing holes.

The Weddell seal's diving ability is exceptional among Antarctic seals, but it has been matched and even exceeded by the northern elephant seal. This apparently ponderous species is an underwater athlete, capable of penetrating depths of nearly 3,000 ft (914 m) in search of deepwater and bottom-dwelling fish and squid, although more normally it dives to 1,150–2,130 ft (350–650 m). Like the Weddell seal, it tends to restrict these adventures to the summer daylight hours, yet even on the brightest day the visibility at such depths is barely adequate, and prey analysis indicates that the seal feeds mainly on bioluminescent species that glow with self-generated light in the submarine gloom. The same phenemonon may be exploited by other seals, particularly the squid-eating Ross seal, which uses its huge eyes to search for squid under the Antarctic sea ice.

USING ITS SENSES

There is some evidence that many seals use a form of echolocation for navigating and finding food. This technique involves producing a series of sound pulses and monitoring the echoes they generate. A distant object may show up as a faint echo returning after a relatively long time delay, while a nearby object will produce a virtually immediate, loud echo. In animals such as insectivorous bats, the system has been refined to create a detailed sound image of the animal's surroundings in complete darkness. This would be invaluable to a seal living beneath the polar ice, where the light is poor at the best of times and dwindles to 24-hour darkness in winter.

Touch is also important. In the Arctic the bearded seal feeds almost entirely on bottom-living fish, crabs, shrimps, clams, and other mollusks, using its luxuriant whiskers to locate food in the poor visibility. The whiskers of all seals are extremely sensitive and probably respond to the water currents set up by passing animals, enabling seals to detect potential prey and even discern the difference between edible shellfish and inedible stones and other debris. Despite this, the bearded seal suffers from worn

Kim Westerskov/Oxford Scientific Films

SUPER SIEVES
The crabeater's teeth mesh together to form a sieve to strain krill from the sea (below).

It is frozen dinner à l'Antarctica for this Weddell seal as it lands a large cod (above).

The charts below show the contrasting diets of the crabeater seal (top) and the leopard seal.

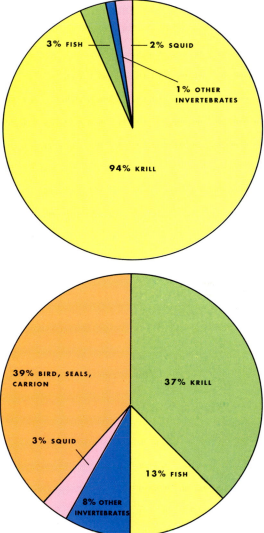

3% FISH

2% SQUID

1% OTHER INVERTEBRATES

94% KRILL

39% BIRD, SEALS, CARRION

37% KRILL

3% SQUID

13% FISH

8% OTHER INVERTEBRATES

FEEDING NICHES

Closely related species often have slightly different diets that enable them to live in the same places without competing with one another. These differences are an integral part of the evolutionary process, since when a particular group of animals begins to exploit a new food resource, it is likely to acquire adaptations for the job. The crabeater seal, for example, has become a specialist at straining krill from the sea, while the leopard seal has acquired the strength to subdue large animals—often crabeaters. In this way both species can thrive in the same waters, although hardly in perfect harmony.

Main illustration Robin Budden

and broken teeth, for many of the animals it eats have stout shells.

The bottom-feeding habit of the bearded seal enables it to thrive alongside other species such as the ribbon seal, which feeds mainly on midwater fish, and the ringed seal, which has a taste for planktonic crustaceans. Similarly the Antarctic species have particular feeding niches that enable them to coexist in the same areas; for while the Weddell seal and Ross seal feed mainly on fish and squid respectively, the crabeater seal feeds almost exclusively on krill, the planktonic crustaceans that swarm in vast clouds in the rich Antarctic seas. The crabeater probably locates krill by touch rather than by sight, employing its whiskers in much the same way as the bearded seal. Unlike other seals, however, the crabeater has no need to locate individual animals and catch them; it simply scoops up seawater by the mouthful and strains it through its teeth to filter out the teeming crustaceans. Its teeth have become highly specialized for the job, with elaborate serpentine cusps; when the seal closes its jaws, the teeth interlock to form an ivory mesh as efficient as any net. Its archenemy the leopard seal has similar meshed teeth that it may use in the same way, but the cusps are stronger and sharper for gripping and dealing with far more substantial prey, such as the crabeaters themselves and penguins.

THE CUNNING KILLER

In a sense, all seals are hunters. To a fish any seal is a major predator, as deadly as a shark. Yet while the predatory abilities of most seals are perfectly adequate for catching fish, they seem modest compared to those of the murderous leopard seal.

Massively built, powerful, and cunning, the leopard seal is the only high-profile predator among the true seals. In fact, apart from the killer whale, it is the only sea mammal that regularly preys on other mammals and birds. In the Antarctic Ocean, where it is widely distributed in the pack ice zone surrounding Antarctica, it is the primary threat to other seals and penguins, and many crabeater seals bear the scars of a leopard seal attack. Yet the fact that so many escape shows that the leopard seal is far from invincible. Like all seals it is an opportunist, and it has few adaptations for dedicated slaughter. Often, particularly when it is young, it feeds on fish and krill, straining the krill out of the seawater in the same way as the crabeater.

WAITING IN AMBUSH

Leopard seals spend a lot of their time patrolling the open water along the edges of shelf ice and between ice floes, occasionally rearing up to scan the ice surface for potential victims. But their main

weapon is surprise, and once a leopard seal is satisfied that there is prey in the vicinity, it tends to sink down out of sight to await its chance.

In early summer the newly weaned crabeater pups are the prime target. Inexperienced and still clumsy in the water, they are relatively easy prey for a determined leopard seal as they make their first exploratory forays in the water. Pups have been seen shooting out of the sea onto ice floes with leopard seals in hot pursuit; once on the ice they are usually safe, for leopard seals are heavy and awkward out of the water. But many pups never make the sanctuary of the ice and are killed and devoured in the water. Curiously the leopard seal often discards the flesh of its victim and eats only the skin and blubber—possibly because the fat complements the protein-rich fish and krill in its diet.

As the summer progresses, the crabeater pups lose their infant clumsiness, becoming more wary and far more difficult to catch. Even if the leopard seal mounts a successful ambush, its victim may still escape by rolling out of the killer's jaws, an action that normally results in two or three deep slashes encircling the crabeater's hide. These scars then stay with the crabeater for life, and some 55 percent of adult crabeater seals are marked in this way. Eventually the crabeaters may become so difficult to catch that the leopard seal will abandon the season's campaign, turning to easier prey such as fish.

PICKING UP A PENGUIN

Some leopard seals specialize in hunting penguins. As with the crabeater kill, this tends to be a seasonal preoccupation that reaches a peak as the young, vulnerable penguins test the water; but even a newly fledged penguin is difficult quarry for a leopard seal. Fast, agile and unpredictable, penguins can only be caught by a surprise attack, often from beneath the ice. A leopard seal will lurk under an ice floe

A leopard seal catches a bite-sized penguin as it tests the water (below). The prey may be small and vulnerable, but the killer leopard seal still depends on surprising its victim by lurking under the ice floe.

Doug Allen/Oxford Scientific Films

Illustration Peter David Scott/Wildlife Art Agency

PENGUIN HUNTING

is a specialized technique that is still somewhat in its infancy (above). *However, as leopard seals evolve, they will probably become more adept at exploiting this abundant food resource.*

as the penguins above prepare to dive into the sea, then shoot out to snatch a victim by the rump. As the other penguins rocket out of the water and back onto the ice, the leopard seal sets about disabling its prize by biting it several times and shaking it vigorously, occasionally ripping its feet off in the process. The penguin generally dies of blood loss and shock within half a minute or so, but the leopard seal keeps thrashing its carcass to and fro in the water to loosen the feather-clad skin and expose the meat beneath; eventually the skin may strip off altogether, like tattered clothing. Small penguins can be swallowed whole, thanks to the seal's adapted windpipe, which collapses to allow bulky food to pass down its gullet; but with bigger penguins the seal eats only the fleshy breast muscles and internal organs.

In general, however, leopard seals have a poor success rate with penguins, and penguin-hunting seems to be limited to a small number of mature, experienced individual seals.   ■

PRIME TARGETS

Newly weaned crabeater seals are vulnerable to attack by leopard seals (left).

1993

TERRITORY

For much of the year many seals lead virtually nomadic lives, roaming through the sea in search of easy prey and hauling out to rest on any convenient ice floes, islands, or secluded beaches. Sometimes seals travel in groups; sometimes they travel alone. Some species such as the harp seal make mass migrations to seasonally rich feeding grounds in the cold polar seas, returning to milder regions to breed. Others stay in the vicinity of their breeding grounds all year, but become widely dispersed as they wander along the coasts and out to sea.

Tracking studies of gray seals in the North Sea indicate that individual seals of the same species vary widely in their movements. Each seal seems to follow its own inclinations, but tends to establish its own pattern of activity.

While some gray seals may forage in loosely defined home ranges of customary haul-out sites, the crabeater seal lives among the continually changing topography of the drifting pack ice. A crabeater might adopt an ice floe as a home base, but the floe could be somewhere else the following day and might break up altogether. Accordingly pack-ice seals tend to be nomads, foraging at will and hitching rides on convenient drifting floes when they need to rest. By contrast, species such as the ringed and Weddell seals that live on the fast ice stay close to breathing holes, which need regular clearing to prevent them from freezing over.

SEASONAL DISPUTES

Seals generally make little attempt to defend favored areas against intruders. Gregarious species such as gray seals, elephant seals, and crabeaters often haul out in close company, and even the unsociable Weddell seal will share its breathing hole

with others—although this occasionally leads to some friction. As the breeding season approaches, however, the males of many species become increasingly territorial, and these territories often take the form of areas of sea. Mature male Weddell seals, for example, defend vast territories below the sea ice. The territory may cover several breathing holes that give access to the ice surface, where breeding females bear the pups conceived during the previous season. When the females disperse after the pups are weaned, they slip down these holes and are immediately waylaid by the resident male. Much the same strategy is employed by the common seal off the northern Atlantic coast.

Among gray seals the situation is slightly different, since gray seals often mate on land. Males may jostle for position in the water off the breeding beach, and a successful male may defend a territory of up to 100 sq miles (259 sq km), but ultimately they move onto the beach itself and attempt to monopolize groups of females in breeding condition. This can lead to trouble as neighboring males fight to retain control of the females they have claimed.

Mark Hamblin/Oxford Scientific Films

Like all true seals, this gray seal (above) moves awkwardly on land, its limbs unable to support its bulk.

INFLATED THREATS

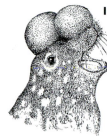

In most true seals the males and females are similar in size and appearance, but in some species polygamous sexual competition has favored larger, more powerful males equipped with special adaptations for intimidating their rivals. Male elephant seals, for example, are vast creatures with elongated, pendulous noses that can be inflated to magnify the seal's image and amplify its roars.

The hooded seal of the northwestern Atlantic is also a polygamous species, but since it breeds on the pack ice where large size confers less advantage, the male is only slightly larger than the female. He compensates for this with a spectacular threat display in which he closes his nostrils and forces air into his nasal cavity, inflating it into a great black balloon on top of his muzzle.

B/W illustrations Ruth Grewcock

BRUTE STRENGTH

To a male elephant seal his "territory" consists of the females he has won access to through a noisy display of brute force (left).

The most spectacular disputes, however, are those of the powerful northern elephant seal, which, like the gray seal, also mates on the beach. As well as being vast, a mature male also has long canine teeth for fighting, a protective shield of armored, wrinkled skin over the neck and chest, and an extended, inflatable proboscis resembling an elephant's trunk. When inflated, this "trunk" curves into the seal's mouth, which acts as a resonating chamber for his snorts and roars. These adaptations have come about because the male of this species is the most polygamous of all true seals. ■

Color illustration Robin Boutell/Wildlife Art Agency

LIFE CYCLE

Among marine mammals, only whales and dolphins have become sufficiently specialized for aquatic life to breed at sea. The seals are forced to give birth and, in most species, suckle their pups on shore or on floating ice. Since true seals have become highly adapted to the water in every other way and cannot move efficiently, find food, or even see particularly well on shore, this biological constraint presents them with a problem.

They have tackled the problem in two ways: They choose secluded or remote breeding sites where their onshore vulnerability puts them at less risk, and they have acquired a number of adaptations that reduce the time on shore to a bare minimum. Typically, a female may spend some three weeks ashore during the breeding season, during which she will give birth, suckle her pup to the point where it is weaned, and mate. The record for a quick turnaround is held by the common or harbor seal. When the birth of her pup is imminent, she hauls out on a tidal sandbank or among rocks below the high-water mark and usually produces her pup within a few minutes of arrival. By the time the returning tide reaches them, both mother and newborn pup are ready to go to sea. Unlike most other species, she suckles the pup in the water until it is capable of feeding itself.

Each male may mate with several females, but his interest in them extends no further, and by the time his pups are born he may be far away. This is hardly surprising, for the pups are not born until a whole year later. The actual gestation—the period

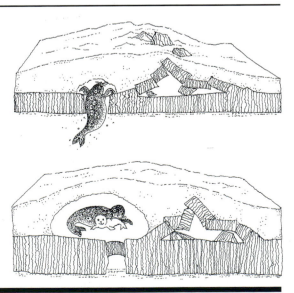

JOSTLING FOR POSITION

About a year after mating, the females are ready to give birth. They haul themselves out onto the pack ice and aggressively set about securing a place on the crowded breeding ground.

SNOW-CAVE NURSERIES

While the harp and hooded seals breed on the unstable pack ice, raising their pups in record time, the ringed seal has its pup on thicker, often permanent or land-fast ice and suckles it in a lair beneath the snow for at least six weeks. The pregnant seals exploit the weaknesses around pressure ridges in the sea ice, digging upward with their foreflippers to create breathing holes. The holes emerge beneath the snow, which often forms deep drifts around the pressure ridges; and each seal hollows out a nursery lair, or often several lairs, beneath the snow cover. The snow shelters the newborn pup from the Arctic windchill and provides some protection against the polar bears and arctic foxes.

B/W illustrations Ruth Grewcock

MATING

During the breeding season males lie in wait beneath the ice floes, ready to mate with females as they enter the water after weaning the newborn pups (above).

A Weddell seal and her newborn pup (right). Weddell seals both breed and give birth on the fast ice around Antarctica.

GROWING UP

The life of a young harp seal

BIRTH

Harp seals, like most ice-breeders, are born with a white lanugo or birth coat, which will eventually be molted.

WEANING

takes place when the pup is between ten and fourteen days old, after which it is abandoned by its mother.

MOLTING

The pup's woolly coat must be molted before it can leave the ice to begin its independent life, foraging at sea.

Rick Price/Survival Anglia

FROM BIRTH TO DEATH	
HARP SEAL	**HAWAIIAN MONK SEAL**
GESTATION: 7.5 MONTHS, AFTER 4 MONTHS DELAYED IMPLANTATION	**GESTATION:** 7.5 MONTHS, AFTER 4 MONTHS DELAYED IMPLANTATION
LITTER SIZE: 1	**LITTER SIZE:** 1
BREEDING: FEBRUARY–MARCH, ON PACK ICE	**BREEDING:** MOSTLY MARCH–MAY
WEIGHT AT BIRTH: 26 LB (12 KG)	**WEIGHT AT BIRTH:** 37 LB (17 KG)
WEANING: 10–12 DAYS	**WEANING:** 40 DAYS
WEIGHT AT WEANING: 73 LB (33 KG)	**WEIGHT AT WEANING:** 140 LB (64 KG)
FIRST ENTERS WATER: 26 DAYS	**FIRST ENTERS WATER:** SOON AFTER BIRTH
SEXUAL MATURITY: 5.5 YEARS	**SEXUAL MATURITY:** 4 YEARS
LONGEVITY: 30 YEARS OR MORE	**LONGEVITY:** 30 YEARS OR MORE

Illustrations Simon Turvey/Wildlife Art Agency

when the pup is developing in the womb—lasts some seven to eight months, but development is suspended at an early stage and the fertilized egg floats freely within the womb instead of becoming attached to the uterine wall. After three to four months, the egg implants and the embryo begins to grow in the normal way. This mechanism, known as delayed implantation, enables the females to take advantage of predator-foiling synchronized birthing and allows both sexes easy access to each other at the pupping sites.

Among many seals the timing of the birth is crucial. Species that breed on the pack ice, such as the harp seal, often start breeding as the weather improves, both to spare their pups the rigors of an Arctic winter and to take advantage of the channels of open water that begin to open up between the ice floes. Before long, however, the spring thaw causes the complete breakup of the ice, destroying the breeding habitat.

There is also every incentive to wean the pup as soon as possible, since in all species except the common seal the pup is suckled out of the water. In the harp seal the pup is suckled for some 10–14 days before being abandoned by its mother; in the hooded seal, which breeds farther offshore on drifting, unstable ice floes, the pup is suckled for an average of only four days—a record among mammals. ■

Blood on the Ice

THE SLAUGHTER OF SEALS FOR THEIR OIL AND HIDES MAY BE HISTORY, BUT SEALS STILL FACE THE WORLDWIDE THREATS OF OVERFISHING, POLLUTION, AND THE DISRUPTION OF THE ENTIRE MARINE ECOSYSTEM

To an Eskimo hunter on the Arctic sea ice, a seal is fair game. The culture of the people is based upon the seal-hunting tradition—a tradition that, for centuries, supplied the necessities of life in one of the harshest climates on Earth. The seal provided meat, hides and furs for clothing, bone and sinew for tools, and oil for heat and light through the long Arctic winter. It was easy to kill, even before the advent of firearms, and a single seal could meet the needs of a large family for some days. Yet even though the Eskimos were engaged in a virtually continuous seal hunt for centuries, they barely made a dent in the great seal populations of the north. Like the polar bears and arctic foxes, they were subsistence hunters, taking just enough for survival.

CULLING FOR COMFORT

The first species of true seals to be exploited for financial profit was the harp seal, which forms large aggregations on easily accessible pack ice in the north Atlantic region in late winter and spring. The earliest commercial hunts were undertaken by Basque whalers off the coasts of Newfoundland in the 16th century, but the first expedition dedicated to the exploitation of the harp seal set out for Jan Mayen Island in 1720. Hunting continued on a modest scale until the 19th century, when booming human populations on both sides of the Atlantic increased the markets for seal products, such as hides and oil, encouraging the seal hunters to step up operations. Altogether some 50 million harp seals have been taken commercially in the 19th and 20th centuries, far more than any other seal, yet somehow the harp seal has weathered this onslaught to survive into the conservation era.

Other species were brought far closer to extinction by the same type of exploitation. In the south Atlantic, the southern elephant seal attracted the attention of whalers looking for a sideline, and following the virtual annihilation of the Antarctic fur seal they began hunting the elephant seals in earnest, clubbing and boiling them down for their valuable oil in great iron try-pots—some of which can still be seen on the subantarctic islands around South Georgia.

Although the market for seal oil more or less evaporated, the market for seal fur remained buoyant, and

Norman Lightfoot/Bruce Coleman Ltd.

Eric & David Hosking/Frank Lane Picture Agency

Until relatively recently, many people were unaware of the barbaric methods used to cull seals (above).

The map below shows the geographic position of the Caspian Sea and Lake Baikal. Both these landlocked lakes have populations of seals.

CASPIAN SEA AND LAKE BAIKAL
(LANDLOCKED LAKES)

LOCKED IN BY LAND

Several species of seals swim up rivers into freshwater, and some have made their homes in landlocked lakes. In the distant past, relatives of the ringed seal colonized Lake Baikal and the Caspian Sea, and these have evolved into distinct species: the Baikal and Caspian seals. These lakes freeze—at least in part—during the winter, enabling the seals to breed on the ice like their arctic relatives, and, although vulnerable to hunters, they have survived until recent times. Today their future is being threatened by pollution, a problem aggravated by the fact that pollutants cannot disperse there as they can in the open sea.

the 1930s saw the start of a valuable trade in the thick infant pelts of northern ice-breeding species, such as the harp seal and hooded seal. This infant lanugo—creamy white in the harp seal, silvery blue-gray in the hooded—is shed soon after lactation ends, so the sealers had to move in on the breeding seals and take their pups while they were still suckling to make sure that the valuable fur was not on the verge of falling out.

Although once exploited, most populations of elephant seals have made a healthy recovery. This one is molting.

This selective form of hunting represented less of a threat than the mass slaughter of former years, but when sealing resumed after a break for World War II, the escalating annual kill—which peaked at 456,000 harp seals in the western Atlantic alone in 1951—led to measurable declines in the seal populations. In the 1960s some 70 percent of the young seals were being killed in the western Atlantic and the Greenland Sea, roughly twice the rate that could be sustained in the long term; and toward the end of the 1960s there were calls for hunting controls purely to conserve the remaining stocks.

In 1967 the issue hit the headlines following the exposure of the barbaric methods used by the hunters. It transpired that they not only clubbed seal pups to death in front of their mothers, but, even worse, frequently skinned pups alive after merely stunning them. The teddy-bear appeal of the pups, still suckling and helpless to defend themselves, ensured maximum public support for the

SEAL CUBS WERE CLUBBED TO DEATH TO SAVE THE COST OF AMMUNITION AND TO ENSURE THAT THE VALUABLE PELTS WERE NOT DISFIGURED BY BULLET HOLES

campaign to stop or at least control the sealers, and within three days of a television broadcast depicting the excesses of the harp seal hunt in the Gulf of St. Lawrence, more than 15,000 complaints were sent to the Prime Minister of Canada.

The complaints proved effective, and the Canadian government was forced to tighten the legal controls over the sealers to ensure that the pups were killed in a humane manner. But the scale of the hunt remained unchecked until 1971, when the main sealing nations (Canada, Norway, and the former Soviet Union) agreed upon a quota system. Meanwhile the market for seal fur had slumped as people became more aware of its distressing origins, and in 1972 the United States prohibited its importation. In 1983 the European Community (EC) followed suit, and four years later the Canadian government banned large-scale commercial exploitation of harp seals.

Unfortunately, legislation enacted in capital cities is difficult to enforce on the pack ice, and in 1989 a new seal scandal broke out when filmed evidence proved that the laws were being systematically flouted by Norwegian sealers, who both grossly exceeded legal quotas and used the barbaric methods outlawed in the late 1960s. It also transpired that infant sealskins were being imported into Europe as "lambskins" to evade the EC ban.

But as if exploitation for profit were not enough, seals are also under attack as a source of economic

Erwin & Peggy Bauer/Bruce Coleman Ltd.

ENDANGERED SPECIES

PARADISE LOST: MEDITERRANEAN MONK SEAL

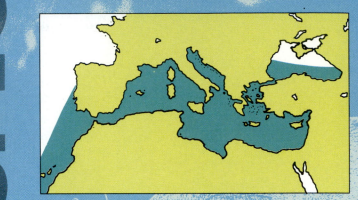

The glittering blue waters of the Aegean are a world away from the icy gray-green of the polar seas, and it may seem extraordinary that seals like those that flourish on the pack ice should live in such a sun-scorched climate. Yet there were probably seals in the Mediterranean long before they colonized the freezing waters of the Arctic and the far south, and until less than 150 years ago the Mediterranean monk seal enjoyed a widespread distribution from the Levant and the Black Sea to Madeira and the Atlantic coast of North Africa. Although locally hunted for their fur, oil, and meat, the seal colonies thrived alongside the human population for thousands of years, and in Greece the sight of monk seals was considered an omen of good fortune for both sailors and fishermen. One of the earliest coins ever discovered, dating from 500 B.C., depicts the head of a monk seal as a symbol of wealth and plenty.

Today, however, much of the wealth of the Mediterranean is derived from tourism, and the tourists are threatening to destroy the

CONSERVATION MEASURES

● Since 1992 the Greek islands of Skiathos, Skopelos, Allonissos, Peristera, Yura, and Piperi have formed the basis of the National Marine Park of the Northern Sporades. The more easterly of these islands are virtually uninhabited, and their secluded coastlines are being conserved as a refuge for the monk seal. Commercial tourism and intensive fishing are prohibited, and the waters around Piperi, the most important breeding site, are

monk seal altogether. Already wiped out from much of its former range by wholesale commercial exploitation during the 19th and early 20th centuries, coupled with persecution by fishermen, the species has been reduced to a scattering of remnant colonies along the coasts of North Africa, Spain, Sardinia, and the eastern Adriatic, a colony on the border of Mauritania and the former state of Western Sahara, and a cluster of colonies in the Aegean and adjacent waters. Altogether these add up to perhaps 500 seals in total, and three-quarters of these have found refuge among the coasts and islands of the Aegean.

THE MEDITERREAN MONK SEAL IS REGARDED AS ONE OF THE TWELVE MOST ENDANGERED MAMMALS IN THE WORLD.

SEALS IN DANGER

THE CHART BELOW SHOWS HOW, IN 1994, THE INTERNATIONAL UNION FOR THE CONSERVATION OF NATURE (IUCN), OR THE WORLD CONSERVATION UNION, CLASSIFIED THE CONSERVATION STATUS OF THE TRUE SEALS THAT ARE KNOWN OR SUSPECTED TO BE UNDER SERIOUS THREAT:

CARIBBEAN MONK SEAL	EXTINCT
MEDITERRANEAN MONK SEAL	ENDANGERED
HAWAIIAN MONK SEAL	ENDANGERED
CASPIAN SEAL	VULNERABLE

EXTINCT MEANS ALMOST CERTAINLY NO LONGER IN EXISTENCE—BARRING A NEAR-MIRACULOUS SURVIVAL IN SOME REMOTE AREA. ENDANGERED MEANS THAT THE SPECIES IS FACING A VERY HIGH PROBABILITY OF EXTINCTION IN THE NEAR FUTURE. VULNERABLE MEANS THAT THE SPECIES IS LIKELY TO DECLINE AND BECOME ENDANGERED IF NOTHING IS DONE TO IMPROVE ITS SITUATION.

Panda/Frank Lane Picture Agency

now a designated "red zone," from which all vessels are prohibited.

● The Bellerive Foundation, headed by the Prince Sadruddin Aga Khan, is building a rehabilitation center for monk seals on the island of Allonissos. The center's main function will be the raising of orphaned or abandoned pups brought in by sympathetic fishermen and tourists.

loss. Fishermen accuse them of stealing fish from nets, damaging nets and other fishing gear, harboring fish parasites, and destroying fish stocks. In recent years marine fish farmers have added to the chorus, accusing seals of killing and damaging the growing fish contained within the net cages. In the North Atlantic ocean, the gray seal and harp seal are seen as the main culprits, but other species have been implicated, including the common seal and, in the Mediterranean, the highly endangered monk seal.

Although there is some truth in the accusations, any shortage of fish in the sea is more likely to be a consequence of gross overfishing by humans. Yet seals are regularly killed on sight by fishermen, and there have been repeated calls for official control policies: in other words, culling the seal herds.

In Great Britain the native gray seal has been legally protected since 1914, courtesy of the Grey Seal Protection Act, which was the first piece of legislation ever passed on behalf of a wild mammal species. Updated in 1932 and 1970, the act prohibits seal hunting during the breeding season, but it contains clauses permitting the culling of seals for fisheries protection. Several such culls have taken place, including a number on the Farne Islands, a designated nature preserve. Paradoxically the action on the Farnes was partly prompted by conservation motives, since rapidly increasing seal numbers threatened the habitat of other species such as puffins. Nevertheless the culling led to protests from the non-fishing public, and in 1977–1978 the last major cull of gray seals in United Kingdom waters, in Orkney, was so effectively opposed by Greenpeace

David Woodfall/NHPA

There are also more insidious threats. Populations of ringed and gray seals in the Baltic are declining, principally because of low birth rates, which have been linked to pollution by certain pesticides. These persistent poisons get into the groundwater, drain into rivers, and ultimately end up in the sea. Since the Baltic is virtually landlocked, the concentrations are particularly high; the chemicals accumulate in the fish that are devoured by the seals, and since the chemicals are soluble in fat, they gradually accumulate in the seals' blubber layers.

TOXIC DUMPING GROUND

Elsewhere pollution of all kinds is proving deadly to seals. The North Sea acts like a dump for the toxic chemicals and heavy metals carried by rivers flowing out of the industrial heartland of Europe, and the epidemic of seal distemper, which decimated the European common seal population in 1988, was probably aggravated by pollution problems. Throughout the world, garbage of all kinds—particularly discarded fish nets—is responsible for innumerable seal deaths. Excess ultraviolet radiation penetrating the gap in the ozone layer above Antarctica—caused by atmospheric pollution—could eventually destroy the krill populations in the Antarctic Ocean, with catastrophic effects for the crabeater seals and, indeed, the whole Antarctic ecosystem. ■

As well as birds and fish, large numbers of seals have died as a result of oil pollution (left).

campaigners that the World Conservation Union forced the government to call it off.

Culling is still a live, emotive issue, particularly in Canada and Norway where the recovering harp seal populations are accused of destroying cod fisheries, but it is probably not a major threat to seal survival. More worrisome is the problem at the root of the culling controversy: the shortage of fish.

In the North Atlantic capelin and sand eels— major prey items for seals—have virtually disappeared in many areas owing to overfishing; the fish famine has caused population crashes among fish-eating seabirds and, although seals can turn to other prey, mass movements of seals in recent years indicate that they are running out of options.

In the Antarctic any attempt to exploit the vast krill swarms of the Antarctic Ocean could seriously threaten the krill-feeding crabeater seal and the leopard seal, not to mention the penguins and other Antarctic species that depend on krill for their survival.

A rescued gray seal convalescing at an RSPCA seal center in Norfolk, England.

Paul Forraby/The Environmental Picture Library

INTO THE FUTURE

If seals could nominate the single most important feature contributing to their survival in the modern world, it could well be their lack of a tear duct. In land mammals this small biological detail serves to drain fluid from the surface of each eye, but since seals live in the water, the duct has been discarded as superfluous. As a result, a seal out of water often appears to be crying as the tears fill its eyes and run down its face. On a wide-eyed, white-coated harp seal pup, the effect can be heartrending, especially when seen in the context of imminent death at the hands of a hunter with a pickax. Flashed around the world in the 1960s and 1970s, photographs of this phenomenon inspired countless people to protest on behalf of the harp seal and, by extension, seals everywhere.

This high conservation profile has done more than earn sympathy for the seals. It has virtually

PREDICTION

THE HUNT GOES ON

In more obscure corners of the Arctic, the commercial seal hunt still goes on, often in blatant contravention of international law. Fortunately, the relentless exposure of the trade by conservation groups may yet force it into submission. Meanwhile, subsistence sealing will continue, but on a scale that does not jeopardize the survival of any seal species.

destroyed the market for their fur, forced a series of humanitarian conservation measures, and blocked a number of potentially damaging seal management policies. It has even brought alternative employment to the people who once earned their living by clubbing seals to death: Out on the pack ice of the Gulf of St. Lawrence, the breeding harp seals have become a tourist attraction. Former sealers now do a brisk trade in catering to the tourists.

Seal hunting may no longer be a serious threat, but, sadly, other problems such as overfishing and pollution are probably out of control. Fish stocks in the northeast Atlantic are at such a low ebb that whole seal populations have moved elsewhere in search of food. ■

RICH PICKINGS

For thousands of years the rich waters of the Antarctic Ocean acted like a magnet for the great baleen whales, vast creatures equipped with enormous sievelike mouths for straining the teeming plankton from the sea. Their main prey was krill: floating shrimplike crustaceans that gather in immense swarms. Jaws agape, the whales would cruise through the swarms like gigantic vacuum cleaners, scooping up krill.

The virtual annihilation of the whales by humans resulted in a huge increase in the quantity of krill available to other species, including fish, penguins, and crabeater seals. The seals responded to the more abundant prey by growing more quickly and maturing earlier. The average age of female maturity apparently fell from four years in 1950 to only 2.5 years by 1980. Earlier maturity means earlier breeding, and therefore a faster rate of breeding in any population. Accordingly, crabeater numbers multiplied, and now they outnumber all the other seal species put together.

ONE BIG FAMILY

Since the last remaining population of 100 or so northern elephant seals was granted total protection in 1922, the species has made a spectacular recovery. Spreading north and south from its island refuge off Baja California, it eventually reoccupied nearly all its original range, and by 1989 total numbers were estimated at some 100,000—approximately the number that existed before man started to exploit them. The catch is, however, that because they are all derived from the same very limited stock, they are all related. This lack of genetic diversity may limit their adaptability in the long term and make them more vulnerable to disease.

Illustration Steve Kingston

INDEX

Published by Marshall Cavendish Corporation
99 White Plains Road
Tarrytown, New York 10591-9001

© Marshall Cavendish Corporation, 1997
© Marshall Cavendish Ltd, 1994

The material in this series was first published in the English language by Marshall Cavendish Limited, of 119 Wardour Street, London W1V 3TD, England.

Library of Congress Cataloging-in-Publication Data

Encyclopedia of mammals.
  p. cm.
  Includes index.
  ISBN 0-7614-0575-5 (set)   ISBN 0-7614-0588-7 (v. 13)

  Summary: Detailed articles cover the history, anatomy, feeding habits, social structure, reproduction, territory,
    and current status of ninety-five mammals around the world.
  1. Mammals—Encyclopedias, Juvenile. [l. Mammals—Encyclopedias.] I. Marshall Cavendish Corporation.
  QL706.2.E54 1996
  599'.003—dc20
                                                            96-17736
                                                              CIP
                                                              AC

Printed in Malaysia
Bound in U.S.A.